You, _____ , can have legitimate hope because you hold in your hands the keys to Staying Up, Up, Up in a Down, Down World.

Teaching by Parable

THE PARABLE has always been my favorite method of teaching. The reason is simple. People remember the story, and when they remember the story, they remember the lesson the story provided. For example, the greatest storyteller of all time, the Carpenter from Galilee, told parable after parable. Incidentally two-thirds of them had to do with our physical and financial well-being.

One of my favorite parables is that told by Dr. Dale E. Turner titled "The Lamplighter:"

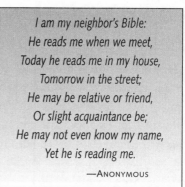

I am my neighbor's Bible:
He reads me when we meet,
Today he reads me in my house,
Tomorrow in the street;
He may be relative or friend,
Or slight acquaintance be;
He may not even know my name,
Yet he is reading me.
—ANONYMOUS

Some people come into our lives and quickly go. Some stay for awhile and leave footprints on our hearts—and we're never ever the same.

Sir Harry Lauder, the Scottish humorist and singer,

loved to tell about an old lamplighter in the village where he lived as a boy. Each evening as dusk came, the old man would make his rounds with his ladder and his light. He would put the ladder against the lamppost, climb up and light the lamp, step back down, pick up the ladder, and proceed to the next lamp.

"After awhile," said Sir Harry, "he would be down the street and out of sight. But I could always tell which way he had gone from the lamps he had lighted and the glow he left behind."

Life's highest tribute would be to live in such a way as to deserve the words, "I could always tell which way he went by the light he left behind."

Like the lamplighter, each one of us leaves a trail wherever we go. Our responsibility—and surely our objective—is to leave a trail we would be willing for our sons and daughters to follow and, in the process, make our parents proud of the trail they left for us. Leave a good trail, and not only will your life be good, but so will the lives of those who follow.

I am secure underneath the protecting shadow of God's Wings and His strong right arm. (Ps. 63:7-8)

So far, you're doing well at following the suggestions. Now read pages 1–2, which explain how to get the most out of this book.

Zig Ziglar

Staying Up, Up, Up in a down, down world

OLIVER
NELSON
TM

THOMAS NELSON PUBLISHERS
Nashville

Library of Congress Control Number: 00-091231

ISBN 0-7852-7077-9

Printed in the United States of America

1 2 3 4 5 6 BVG 05 04 03 02 01 00

To the memory of John R. Anderson

*My first male nonfamily role model
who taught and lived with integrity.*

*He became my surrogate father
and treated me like a son.*

Other books by Zig Ziglar

Over the Top
Confessions of a Grieving Christian
Something to Smile About
Something Else to Smile About

Contents

Week Twenty-Four

Week Twenty-Five

Week Twenty-Six

About the Author

Preface

PSYCHIATRIST ALFRED ADLER said that hope is the foundational quality of all change. It is also the great activator. People with hope take action to realize their dreams. People without hope are often so discouraged, they feel incapable of doing anything significant. Good news: hope and help are available—that's what this book is about.

Somebody once remarked, "Life is so 'daily.'" The implication is clear: there are so many obstacles to overcome that the daily grind of life has a tendency to be a hope killer. *Staying Up, Up, Up in a Down, Down World* is designed to give you hope, direction, and encouragement *every* day. Since each day is a part of every lifetime, you will have a hope-filled and, hence, a happier, more productive life when you put all your hope-filled days together. No, that doesn't mean life will be trouble-free, but it does mean you will handle problems (opportunities) in a different and more effective manner. This approach is simple, but it's not simplistic. It's based on the power of God and an understanding of advanced mathematics: you + God = enough.

Question: When do you need hope? *Answer:* Every day. Since encouragement is the fuel on which hope runs, this book is designed to give you hope and encouragement every day.

In every vignette of *Staying Up, Up, Up in a Down, Down World* I will conclude the message with scripture that I've personalized and put into the first person, present tense (much like the Twenty-third Psalm). Some will deal with God's promises, some with our responsibilities.

One reason I love gospel music and the beautiful old hymns is that they verbalize—in the first person, present tense—God's promises and emphasize His love for me. Because His presence is assured, His greatness is extolled, and His love is expressed, His comforting presence and peace of mind become integral parts of my life. I hope His comforting presence and peace of mind become integral parts of your life as well.

Using *Staying Up, Up, Up in a Down, Down World*

MANY GOOD STUDENTS are not good thinkers. For maximum benefit from this book, read one story each day, then think about—and, if possible, talk about—what you read. Each parable has a purpose. When you combine reading, thinking, and talking about the parables included here, you will find balance because I deal with the physical, mental, and spiritual. I involve the personal, family, career, and financial aspects of life. All are important.

Patience, discipline, and focus are the keys. Study one message—and one message only—each day. It takes about three minutes to read and print on a three-by-five-inch card the biblical self-talk at the end of each one. Start your day with one vignette. Read the biblical self-talk aloud, and quietly read it again several times during the day. At the end of the day, read the story again, and stand before a mirror, look yourself in the eye, and read the self-talk out loud.

Think about it. If you start the day properly, end the day properly, and include the family in between, doesn't it make sense that everybody's day will be better?

1

Some messages are excellent to use in five- to ten-minute staff meetings or to share with the family after a meal. Read the story aloud, then discuss it for a few minutes. For most families, doing this every day will be impossible, but benefits will be excellent if you manage to do this once or twice each week.

Psychologists say our first encounter of the day has significant impact on the rest of our day. We also know that the last thing we put into our minds at night will be the thing we will dwell on, even as we sleep. This procedure will make your day more joyful and your night more restful.

I'm convinced that if you follow this procedure each week, by the time you have finished the book you will have made serious progress toward a better future because you are staying up, up, up in a down, down world.

Week One

Who's Who in America

SEVERAL YEARS AGO the people listed in *Who's Who in America* were analyzed. Researchers discovered that it took 25,000 laboring families to produce 1 child who would be listed in *Who's Who*. It required 10,000 families in which the father was a skilled craftsman, 6,000 Baptist preachers, 5,000 lawyers, 5,000 Presbyterian preachers, 2,500 dentists, and 1,200 Episcopalian priests to produce someone listed in *Who's Who*.

However, every 7 Christian missionary families produced a member of *Who's Who*. I can only speculate on the reasons for the remarkable difference. Surely most of the preachers from the various denominations were men and women of faith, but I believe the missionaries, in most cases,

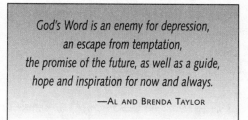

God's Word is an enemy for depression,
an escape from temptation,
the promise of the future, as well as a guide,
hope and inspiration for now and always.

—AL AND BRENDA TAYLOR

demonstrated a stronger commitment. Their example demonstrated their faith and courage to their children. Also, they probably did not have many things to give to their children, but the mother and father, with fewer distractions such as daily newspapers and television, were probably spending an unusual amount of time with them. The kids had a day-to-day example and a chance to study what real success was all about. Needless to say, the parents were teaching and preaching the Bible every day and felt a unique relationship with God through the person of Jesus Christ. Undoubtedly the role modeling and demonstration of their faith played a significant part in the development of the children.

All of us have heard that we teach what we know, but we reproduce what we are, which is exactly what God tells us in Luke 6:40 (NKJV): "A disciple is not above his teacher, but everyone who is perfectly trained will be like his teacher." My mother repeatedly said to me as a young father, "Son, your children pay more attention to what you do than to what you say."

In many cases, the missionary family had to learn to communicate in a different language from their native language and get along with people of different cultures, which brought about a maturing of the youngsters. Then when the kids returned to America to live, they had a chance to view the difference in the opportunities in America, and they capitalized on those opportunities.

I am becoming wise because I have taken the first step, which is to trust and reverence the Lord. I also have listened to my father and mother, and honors are coming my way. (Prov. 1:7–9)

Those Dull Sermons

SINCE CHILDHOOD I've heard countless little funnies and many criticisms of the dull sermons some preachers deliver on a regular basis to their congregations. It's more than just a cliché to say that some of them really will put you to sleep! As one person described it: "Preaching is the art of talking in someone else's sleep," or "We start at eleven o'clock sharp and end at twelve o'clock dull."

One pastor said, "When my deacons fall asleep while I'm preaching, I just see it as a vote of confidence that I won't say anything heretical." That's a positive way of looking at it! And think about this: the sleeping one might be creating something good.

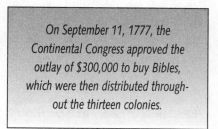

On September 11, 1777, the Continental Congress approved the outlay of $300,000 to buy Bibles, which were then distributed throughout the thirteen colonies.

In 1974 at the North Presbyterian Church in North St. Paul, Minnesota, one member of the congregation was Art Fry, who was having trouble focusing on the sermon, so he started to daydream. This 3M scientist was frustrated because he could not mark the hymnbooks without making a big mess. He devoted considerable thought to that and used the sermon time to figure out a solution. That was the day he invented Post-it Notes.

I'm not certain that Art told the preacher what he was doing during the sermon, but I know that his company and millions of Americans are glad he was putting the time to practical use. So the next time you see somebody dozing during a sermon, just remember that he might be coming up with the next hula hoop or Post-it Notes.

Personally I'm grateful that in the church I attend, anybody who closes his eyes is either dead or dead tired. Dr. Jack Graham and our music department keep things hopping with exciting, usable, lifesaving eternity information and inspiration. On occasion I have attended dull church services and heard dull sermons, but I have never attended a dull worship service. How can you make Jesus Christ, the Creator of the universe, dull? You could never do that with the Christ I know. How could you make the One who healed the sick, raised the dead, stilled the waters, and died for my sins dull?

As a child of God, I listen to Him and put into practice what I hear so God reveals to me the things I need to do and understand. He hides these things from the nonbeliever and the believer who does not do what God has revealed. (Mark 4:22–25)

Persistence Pays

THE MARCH 16, 1998, issue of *USA Today* featured an article about dieting in America. It seems that after twenty years of diet, exercise, miracle potions, and a host of gimmicks, the American people have concluded that losing weight is a lost cause for them. They take it off and put it back on. They are unhappy losing the weight, depriving themselves of their favorite foods, and then feeling guilty because they regain the weight. There's a major trend among millions of Americans who are saying, "To heck with it! I'm going to eat what I want and just suffer the consequences, but I'm not going to be miserable about it."

That's an unfortunate approach. But I understand why they feel that way because for many years I was on that roller coaster. A quarter of a century ago I decided to lose weight on a gradual basis, and in a ten-month period of eating sensibly and exercising regularly, I lost thirty-seven pounds. I averaged losing one and nine-tenths ounces per day.

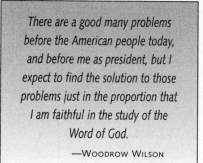

There are a good many problems before the American people today, and before me as president, but I expect to find the solution to those problems just in the proportion that I am faithful in the study of the Word of God.

—WOODROW WILSON

I'll bet you just said to yourself (if you have a weight problem), "I could do that."

Most attempts at weight loss are undermined by unrealistic promises made about a "revolutionary" new approach or product that "will take all the weight off permanently and you won't even feel hungry." The real answer is a change of lifestyle, a combination of eating sensibly and exercising regularly. Benefits are enormous. On November 24, 1999, at age seventy-three, I stayed on the treadmill at the Aerobics Center more than two minutes longer than I was able to stay at age forty-five when I weighed over 200 pounds and was terribly out of shape. I have a resting heart rate of 47, my cholesterol level was described by Dr. Larry Gibbons, the examining physician, as "perfect" at 156, and my blood pressure is 110/60. Those are the readings typical of a much younger man. And my enthusiasm for life grows every day.

I am always joyful and I always keep praying. I am always thankful, no matter what happens, for this is God's will for me because I belong to Christ Jesus alone. (1 Thess. 5:16-18)

Don't Be a Puritan Basher

I HAVE LONG been amused and amazed but more often puzzled and even irritated at some of the comments made concerning the Puritans who settled in New England. Several years ago I read the best book I've read in my adult life, *The Light and the Glory* by David Manuel and Peter Marshall. It really is the true history of America. The authors went to the libraries at Yale and Harvard Universities and read hundreds of original sermons that in those days were meticulously handwritten.

Based on their research, these men painted an entirely different picture of the Puritans. They were far more funloving than they've been accused of being, but they insisted that the pleasures of the flesh be subordinated for and to the greater glory of God. They were not ascetics, and they never even hinted that they wanted to deny or prevent the enjoyment of earthly pleasures.

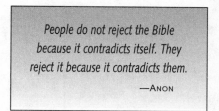

People do not reject the Bible because it contradicts itself. They reject it because it contradicts them.

—ANON

Those people practiced the golden rule and shared anything they had with those who were less fortunate than they. They gave out of the very little they had, not out of an abundance. *Worldly*

9

Saints, by Wheaton College's Leland Ryken, notes that Puritanism was a youthful, highly educated movement. The Puritans revived Cambridge University and founded Harvard only six years after founding the Massachusetts Bay Colony.

An article in the *Wall Street Journal* on March 4, 1998, stated that the Puritans consistently extolled sex within marriage. William Gouge was typical in calling sex "one of the most proper and essential acts of marriage," to be enjoyed "with goodwill and delight, willingly, readily, and cheerfully." One congregation even excommunicated a man for sexually neglecting his wife.

The conclusion I reached is this: if we all followed more of the Puritans' examples, we would have happier marriages, and even more to smile about and be grateful for.

My God-given wisdom gives me a long, good life, riches, honor, pleasure, peace, and living energy. (Prov. 3:16–18)

Alligators and People

A ZOO REVEALS an interesting quirk of human nature.

Although you generally go to the zoo to see and learn about animals, you will learn much about people if you visit the alligator exhibit at the zoo in Houston, Texas. In no other cage will you find as many coins of all sizes and from several nations scattered throughout.

Why? The possible answer lies in the sign posted near the alligator habitat by the Zoological Society requesting that money *not* be thrown into the alligators' water because it takes only one coin, ingested by an alligator, to eventually kill it.

It seems that human nature is to rebel against authority. Incidentally, coins are thrown by adults as well as children, so we can't blame the coin tossing on the

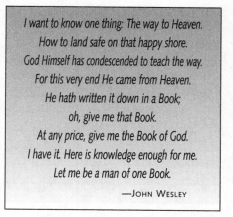

I want to know one thing: The way to Heaven.
How to land safe on that happy shore.
God Himself has condescended to teach the way.
For this very end He came from Heaven.
He hath written it down in a Book;
oh, give me that Book.
At any price, give me the Book of God.
I have it. Here is knowledge enough for me.
Let me be a man of one Book.

—JOHN WESLEY

rebellion of youth. The unfortunate thing about this act of rebellion is that until we learn how to obey, we will never know how to lead. It's safe to say that most laws and rules passed in a democracy or an institution are for the overall good of the majority of the people. In this case they certainly are for the good of the alligators and ultimately for the good and enjoyment of the thousands who visit the zoo.

If an individual who threw a coin into the alligator habitat observed an alligator ingesting the coin and later returned to watch it die as a result, he would probably feel sadness and say, "I wish I hadn't done that."

I am happy because I am strong in the Lord and want above all else to follow His steps. (Ps. 84:5)

Week Two

It's Ironic

ST. PATRICK'S DAY honors the monk who took Christianity to Ireland. Unfortunately, as an article by John Lang for Scripps Howard News Service puts it, "St. Patrick's Day has emerged as one of the deadliest days in the United States and is an unholy ritual of drunkenness." He goes on to say, "There is a higher percentage of traffic deaths related to alcohol on this day than any other day of the year."

Nearly 63 percent of accidents on St. Patrick's Day relate to alcohol abuse. By comparison, according to the National Highway Traffic Safety Administration, alcohol-related accidents total 52 percent on New Year's Day, 51 percent on Memorial Day, 47 percent on the Fourth of July, 46 percent on Thanksgiving, and about 40 percent on an ordinary day of the week.

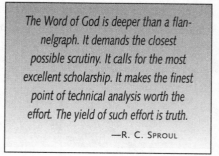

The Word of God is deeper than a flannelgraph. It demands the closest possible scrutiny. It calls for the most excellent scholarship. It makes the finest point of technical analysis worth the effort. The yield of such effort is truth.

—R. C. SPROUL

It's truly sad that we've made celebrating the holidays an excuse to consume large amounts of alcoholic beverages with the inevitable results. We need to think about several things. Perhaps one reason New Year's resolutions are so often broken is that a high percentage of them are made under the influence of alcohol. Then I question if consuming alcohol on Memorial Day is the proper way to honor the men and women who have given their lives for our freedom. On the Fourth of July, celebrating our freedom as a nation should be a sobering moment, as should our celebration of Thanksgiving Day when we are reminded of God's goodness to the pilgrims and His continued bountiful provisions for us today.

The *1828 Noah Webster Dictionary* says that to *celebrate* is "to praise, to commend, to make famous, to distinguish by solemn rites, to keep holding, to honor or distinguish by ceremonies and marks of joy and respect." That doesn't seem to say anything about getting drunk, does it? I'm convinced that if we celebrate (according to its original intent) with sobriety, more people will have longer to celebrate many good things.

I rejoice because my trust is in You. I shout for joy because You defend me. I love Your name , so I am joyful in You. (Ps. 5:11)

Needed: A Moral Compass

PEOPLE ARE ASKING more and more often, "Have we lost our moral direction in America?" The answer seems to be clear that if we have not lost it, we are certainly headed in that direction.

A poll taken in 1990 revealed that 17 percent of employees believed it was okay to involve themselves in at least minor theft from their employers. In 1998, that figure had risen to 37 percent. Pollster George Gallup Jr., whose organization has been conducting this kind of research for more than fifty years, said, "We now have people debating the relevance of the Ten Commandments. Is the first one applicable? Two? Three or four? Should we ignore the one on adultery? Is bearing false witness really lying?"

According to Gallup, in 1969, 68 percent of the population believed it was morally wrong to have premarital sex.

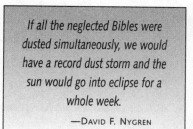

> If all the neglected Bibles were dusted simultaneously, we would have a record dust storm and the sun would go into eclipse for a whole week.
>
> —DAVID F. NYGREN

In 1996, the figure was down to 40 percent. In 1999 approximately 70 percent of Americans gave President Clinton a high rating on his job effectiveness, 39 percent said they strongly disapproved of the moral example he set for the country, and only 14 percent said they "strongly approved."

The ethicists can argue all they want. There are some moral absolutes. My mother explained the difference between right and wrong with an analogy: "When you break a rotten egg, you won't have to ask anyone if it's good or bad. You'll just know because the odor will be very convincing."

John Lummox asserted, "Character is the keystone of life. Character means the quality of the stuff of which anything is made. We can learn from others what is needed for character, but the actual carving we must do ourselves."

Solution: parents should teach their children from birth the values of honesty, character, and integrity. They should encourage them to go to their house of worship regularly and join the Boy or Girl Scouts where these values are taught. It's still true, again as my mother used to say, "As the twig is bent, so shall the tree grow."

The Lord is my shield and protects me from the wicked [God's promise]. When I am slipping, I scream for help [my responsibility], and He saves me [God's promise]. (Ps. 94:16–18)

The Land of Opportunity

FOR MANY YEARS I've been waving the flag, extolling the virtues of the opportunities that America has to offer. Stories are legendary about people who start with nothing and end up being ultrasuccessful, not only financially but also in the positions they occupy as independent businesspeople or corporate executives, as well as being successful at home in their personal and family lives.

Surely one of the better success stories is that of Michael Quinlan, who at one time was a mailroom clerk earning two dollars an hour. For over a decade he was the

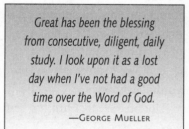

Great has been the blessing from consecutive, diligent, daily study. I look upon it as a lost day when I've not had a good time over the Word of God.

—GEORGE MUELLER

CEO of McDonald's. When he was under the microscope because McDonald's had not made the progress the company had anticipated, there were those who speculated that if he couldn't improve his performance, he would retire or "get the boot" because his job was on the line.

Quinlan responded that his job was always on the line, but it didn't seem to bother him because he was in the process of making changes, as all successful people must do.

Two major points: Michael Quinlan had an inauspicious start but at age forty-three was made CEO of a multibillion-dollar corporation. He's a solid family man with two sons and two grandchildren. He shoots bogey golf and enjoys deep-sea fishing. In short, he's a man who is able to enjoy a balanced lifestyle. This is an area in which many people deny themselves. It's the same old saw: "I don't have the time." I'm going to suggest that it's not lack of time, but lack of direction. When we prioritize our "got to do's" and include our "need to do's" and "want to do's," we discover that just as we do on the day before vacation, we get a lot more done. However, we must plan those things, or nothing is going to happen. No, it's not lack of time—it's lack of direction that makes the difference. Michael Quinlan has his priorities in order, and his direction includes his family, which gives him a balanced life.

It doesn't make any difference where you start; it's where you go that counts.

Update: While Quinlan remains on the board of directors, he was succeeded as CEO on May 20, 1999, by Michael M. Greenburg.

I lie down in peace and sleep, for You alone, O Lord, always keep me safe. (Ps. 4:8)

Not to Change Is Stressful

WE FREQUENTLY hear that "people refuse to change because change is stressful." I would like to suggest that not to change is even more stressful because the world is changing.

Let's start with the business world. In 1917, the one hundred largest corporations in America were identified, and in 1998, only fifteen of them were still in business. They disappeared entirely or merged with or were bought out by other companies. One of the companies I represented for eight years refused to change, and as a result it went under and was eventually taken over. It sold an excellent product, but when new develop-

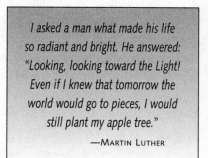

I asked a man what made his life so radiant and bright. He answered: "Looking, looking toward the Light! Even if I knew that tomorrow the world would go to pieces, I would still plant my apple tree."

—MARTIN LUTHER

ments entered the field, the company stuck by the original product and the consumers took their business elsewhere.

Many marriages have been saved because the spouses were willing to change their attitudes and behaviors. On the other hand, countless marriages have failed because the spouses refused to make any changes at all, indulged in "the blame

19

game," and created intolerable conditions under which no one could live.

Many people who have difficulty keeping jobs end up unemployed because they are unwilling to change. From my perspective the word *change* means "to grow," or "to change from doing the wrong thing to doing the right thing." On the growth perspective, Eric Hoffer said it extremely well: "In times of change the learners shall inherit the earth, while the learned find themselves beautifully equipped to deal with a world that no longer exists." To that, Tom Peters added, "Only those who constantly retool themselves stand a chance of staying employed in the years ahead." Yes, continuing to grow eliminates a lot of stress and builds employment security.

Charles Gow summed it up: "The two great laws of life are growth and decay. When things stop growing, they begin to die. This is true of men, business or nations."

I trust and reverence the Lord [my responsibility]. My reward is prosperity and happiness. My wife is contented in our home, and my children are vigorous and healthy. (Ps. 128:1–4)

Example Is Still the Best Teacher

THIS EVENT RECALLED by a missionary's daughter took place many years ago:

> To celebrate the coming of Christian missionaries to a region of Zaire, a daylong event was filled with speeches, testimonies, and music.

> That rally is best remembered for the way it ended. A very old man came before the crowd and insisted he be allowed to speak. He said his death was imminent, and if he did not speak now the information he carried might never be known. He explained that when missionaries first came a century ago, his people did not trust them. They were unusual and had a strange message. The tribal leaders.decided to test the missionaries by slowly poisoning them

> *Let mental culture go on advancing, let the natural sciences progress to an even greater extent and depth, and the human mind widen itself as much as it desires; beyond the elevation and moral culture of Christianity as it shines forth in the Gospels, it will not go.*
> —GOETHE

to death. Over the months and years that followed, these tribesmen witnessed the fashion in which death and grief were handled by the missionary families. The old man said, "It was as we watched how they died that we decided that we wanted to live as Christians."

The story was unknown for a hundred years. Those who died painful, strange deaths were never certain why they were dying or what impact their lives would have. Through it all, though, they stayed and preached their strange message.

The best recipe for happiness and contentment I've seen is this: dig a big hole in the garden of your thoughts and put into it all your disillusions, disappointments, regrets, worries, troubles, doubts, and fears. Cover well with the earth of fruitfulness. Water it from the well of contentment. Sow on top the seeds of hope, courage, strength, patience, and love. Then when the time for gathering comes, may your harvest be a rich and fruitful one.

I trust and reverence the Lord and turn my back on evil, so He directs me, gives me success, and gives me renewed health and vitality. (Prov. 3:5–8)

Week Three

Gratitude Is Possible

HELEN KELLER REMARKED, "I have always thought it would be a blessing if each person could be blind and deaf for a few days during his early adult life. Darkness would make him appreciate sight; silence would teach him the joys of sound."

Actually, Helen Keller understated the case. All of us would be truly grateful for the ability to use the senses she spoke of. According to the 1828 Noah Webster dictionary, grateful means "having a due sense of bene-fits, kindly disposed

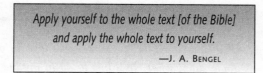

Apply yourself to the whole text [of the Bible] and apply the whole text to yourself.

—J. A. BENGEL

towards one from whom a favor has been received; it's agreeable, pleasing, acceptable, gratifying, and is a grateful present."

One reason I'm such a flag-waving American and have been all of my life is that I've had the privilege of seeing virtually every kind of condition known to man in my lifetime. I've been in East Berlin when the Communists were in control and seen the expressionless faces and eyes of the people, as well as block after block of empty stores and parking spaces on a main thorough-fare. I've been into Third World countries and seen unbelievable poverty—small children with no clothes to wear, emaciated bodies, filthy, muddy streets where people lived in squalor that most Americans cannot even imagine. I've also seen luxury on one side of a highway and abject poverty on the other side.

Yes, I know we have slums in America and many people suffer some of the things I've described, but no laws or walls keep people there. I've seen and talked to many homeless people who, a year later, were gainfully employed and living in acceptable housing.

All of this is to say that I'm most grateful for the opportunity America affords so that anyone with a little encouragement and internal drive can move onward and upward. It behooves all of us to remember that the more we express gratitude for what we have, the more we will have to express gratitude for.

The Holy Spirit has given me great love for others. God helps me understand what He wants to do in my life and makes me wise about spiritual things. (Col. 1:8–9)

They're Not All Bad

THERE'S BEEN a lot of flak concerning high-paid professional athletes and their negative behavior. For example, Latrell Sprewell, a multimillion-dollar athlete, attacked his coach not once but twice. Incredibly enough, he was "vindicated" by arbitrator John D. Feerick, a highly respected dean at Fordham University Law School, who made what virtually everyone considered a bad decision. As a result, people were outraged because they feared the decision opened the door for even more outrageous conduct.

However, let me point out a very positive example, center fielder Marquis Grissom of the Milwaukee Brewers. He is the fourteenth of fifteen children, and he, too, received a multimillion-dollar contract. In his case, he recognized the encouragement his family had given him over the years, and he bought homes for eleven of his brothers and sisters. This is truly a class act and a wonderful way of thanking them for their support.

> If I were the devil, one of my first aims would be to stop folk from digging into the Bible.
>
> —J. I. PACKER

Then turn to the story of Ben Agajanian, one of the most respected kicking coaches of all time. He has trained many legendary NFL kickers, and at age eighty he's still going strong. Every year Agajanian conducts kicking clinics all around the Dallas area for kids and adults who want to improve their careers. What does Agajanian get out of it? His rewards go considerably beyond the financial ones. He said, "Seeing the kids get college scholarships is a big motivation for me." He gets a thrill out of helping youngsters get their chance in life.

It has been said that you can tell a big person by the way he treats a little one. That means we can tell the true measure of a person of stature and/or influence by how he deals with someone who, because of age or circumstances beyond his control, has not accomplished a great deal with his life. I'm confident that Marquis Grissom and Ben Agajanian are thrilled to do what they can to help those who are less fortunate than they are. I'll also bet they get a double-extra charge out of it, as they've indicated in what they've said, by watching the gleam in the eyes, the joy in the hearts, and the appreciation in the souls of those who are lifted by their selfless examples.

I am happy because I am strong in the Lord and want above all else to follow His footsteps. (Ps. 84:5)

Those Statistical Lies

A WELL-KNOWN "fact" is that 50 percent of all the people who marry in America end up divorced. But is it a fact, or is it one of those statistics that has not been properly presented? And if it has not been properly presented, why do we continue to present it?

One possible reason is that somehow it makes divorce less threatening. After all, if half of the people who get married end up divorced, then people can say, "I'm not really that different from others." That line of thinking sometimes encourages divorce, which in many cases could be avoided with a change in thinking and the way spouses deal with each other.

> I have known 95 of the world's great men in my time, and of these 87 were followers of the Bible. The Bible is stamped with a specialty of origin and an immeasurable distance separates it from all competitors.
> —WILLIAM E. GLADSTONE

Census Bureau records conclusively prove that the statistical data are incorrect. A newly created category enables statisticians to track everyone who has been married and everyone who has been divorced. As a result, some exciting and encouraging information has been revealed. According to these figures, less than 20 percent of the people who get married end up divorced. The 50 percent figure includes those who have been divorced multiple times, and individuals who have been divorced three, four, five, or more times skew the statistics to an incredible degree.

The good news is, 80 percent of people who marry end up staying married until death parts them. So when you start thinking in terms of marriage, think in terms of the odds being five to one that it's going to be permanent. You can increase those odds by careful courtship: date your intended two or more years before you marry, and come to know not only the individual but also the family.

In the process, you should make it a habit to say something nice to and about each other every day. A sincere compliment goes a long way. Praise the good qualities of your mate as a way of life. Learn to laugh at life and *with* each other, not *at* each other. Be kind, considerate, and thoughtful. A rule for wives to follow is to be as nice to your husband as you are to your hairdresser; husbands, be as considerate of and conversant with your wife as you are to a stranger on the street seeking directions. To this add your commitment to work on your marriage, no matter what.

I honor my marriage and its vows, and I am pure because I know God will punish me if I am immoral or commit adultery. (Heb. 13:4)

Personality

MY DICTIONARY tells me that *personality* is the "personal or individual quality that makes one person be different and act differently from another." *Personality* is "the total physical, intellectual and emotional structure of an individual, including abilities, interests, and attitudes." Personality is the sum total of all of our qualities. With this in mind, let's explore the benefits and ramifications of a pleasing personality.

Today at lunch in a family restaurant, one of the hostesses came by and, with a pleasant smile, asked us about our meal. We commented that it was delicious, and she said, "I'm really pleased. We're glad you folks are here eating with us." After she left, I commented to my wife that she was certainly a pleasant, personable young woman, and my wife wholeheartedly agreed.

> The Scriptures teach us the best way of living, the noblest way of suffering, and the most comfortable way of dying.
>
> —JOHN FLAVEL

Too many people have forgotten that we can choose to smile and be pleasant or to frown and be rude and thoughtless. Too many people make the wrong choice, and their personalities make them come across as people we don't want as friends or coworkers.

There is only one opportunity to make a first impression, and all of us instinctively make decisions or judgments about an individual within the first few seconds of crossing paths. With that in mind, I believe that when we teach our kids to smile, to be pleasant and cheerful, to be courteous and respectful of others, to pleasantly respond to requests or questions, we are helping them develop a personality that will open many doors for them. Once the doors are opened, only character will keep them open, so it's even more important to give the personality a foundation with character.

I take every opportunity to tell others the good news, and I am wise in all of my contacts with them. My conversation is gracious and sensible, so I have the right answer for everyone. (Col. 4:5–6)

Serving Is His Calling

CUSTOMER SERVICE gets a lot of lip service. However, Geoff Gregor, the manager of special services with American Airlines at the Orange County (John Wayne) Airport in California, takes that term seriously and follows the biblical admonition: "He who would be the greatest among you must become the servant of all."

I first met Geoff when he overheard me requesting an aisle seat. He took it upon himself to ask another passenger, a friend of his, to swap seats with me. It was a brief but pleasant encounter, which indicated that Geoff genuinely tries to meet his customers' requests if humanly possible.

> The Bible, the whole Bible, and nothing but the Bible is the religion of Christ's church.
> —CHARLES HADDON SPURGEON

Geoff apparently scans the passenger lists of flights coming in and going out daily because the next time I flew into Orange County for a speaking engagement, he greeted me personally and welcomed me, as he did several other passengers he also knew by name. I saw him next when he attended the seminar where I spoke, and I admired a tie he was wearing. The following day Geoff met me at my departure gate and told me he wanted to send me the tie I had admired. He shared that someone special to him had given it to him, but he wanted me to have it because I had been special in his life and he felt that a gift that was meaningful to him was more significant. Each time I wear that tie I get numerous compliments, and knowing its significance makes it doubly special.

On January 27, 1998, I again spoke in Orange County, and Geoff was in the audience. When I arrived at the airport to catch my flight back to Dallas, he was waiting. Although I won't tell you the details of what happened (because it's a little too embarrassing), again he came to my rescue, handled the problem without any difficulty, and once more I was on my way home.

What a delight to meet someone like him in this hurry-hurry world of ours! Wouldn't it be wonderful if all of us took that genuine-interest service approach to life and went the extra mile, as Geoff does?

My God-given wisdom brings me a long, good life, riches, honor, pleasure, peace, and living energy. (Prov. 3:16–22)

Week Four

Unlearning What We Learned

THE GOOD NEWS is that whatever we have learned, we can also unlearn, though on occasion that can be more difficult than the learning process itself. For example, the drug abuser had to learn to use drugs and/or alcohol, which in many cases is fairly easy to do. However, once drug or alcohol use becomes a habit, he can still unlearn the habit.

That's important because too many people have learned some things that desperately need unlearning. Research by Professor Don McCabe of Rutgers University, involving 4,300 students at 31 highly selective colleges, 14 of which had honor codes, was reported in the March 11, 1996, issue of *USA Today*. The study updated one that was conducted in

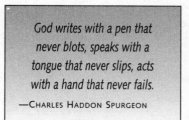

God writes with a pen that never blots, speaks with a tongue that never slips, acts with a hand that never fails.
—CHARLES HADDON SPURGEON

1990 and revealed that 30 percent of students at schools with honor codes in 1995 reported cheating on a test. That's up from 24 percent in 1990. At schools without honor codes, 45 percent in 1995 reported cheating on a test; that's down from 47 percent in 1990. Professor McCabe calls the results "discouraging," a considerable understatement.

Here are two steps that will produce results to reduce the cheating. First, please understand that 80 percent of a child's character is formed by age five, so the example parents set in living consistent lives of integrity and playing according to the rules of the game is a key ingredient. If kids see parents playing it straight and not cheating at home, on the highways, or in their businesses, the kids are far less likely to cheat in school.

Second, starting in kindergarten, important lessons should be taught in our educational institutions about the moral approach to life. The Thomas Jefferson Research Center in Pasadena, California, reports, "Some things are common in all great civilizations and religions—wisdom, integrity, love, freedom, justice, courage, humility, patience, industriousness, thriftiness, generosity, objectivity, cooperation, moderation and optimism." To this list I would add responsibility and dependability. I'm firmly convinced that when these lessons are taught in childhood and reinforced in our educational system, our kids will enter the business world playing it straight—which gives them the best opportunity to move straight to the top.

I do not murder, commit adultery, steal, lie, or envy my neighbor's house, or desire to sleep with His wife or want to own anything that is his. (Ex. 20:13–17)

Trouble Might Be a Good Thing

SEVERAL YEARS AGO Harold S. Kushner wrote the book *When Bad Things Happen to Good People*. Many times we don't understand why bad things happen to good people. A good person may be seriously injured in an automobile accident and a promising athletic career is ended, or a life-threatening, debilitating disease may take away the mobility of that person and disable him for life. For that matter, the loss of a young person's life is extremely difficult to understand. Why does God permit such things to happen?

First, we need to understand that a loving heavenly Father is never going to permit anything to happen to one of His children that is not in his long-range best interests. Romans 8:28 (NKJV) clearly states, "All things work together for good to those who love God, to those who are the called according to His purpose." The meaning is not that everything that happens is good; rather, God takes all the things and puts them together, and they work out for good.

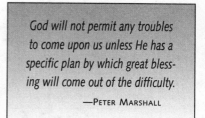

God will not permit any troubles to come upon us unless He has a specific plan by which great blessing will come out of the difficulty.

—PETER MARSHALL

Everyone who has read the Bible knows the story of Joseph.

Jealousy caused his older brothers to sell him into slavery in Egypt, where he rose in the kingdom and became the second in command to Pharaoh. God told Joseph the meaning of Pharaoh's dreams: seven years of feast followed by seven years of famine. Then Joseph stored grain for the seven years of famine that would come. When his brothers came to buy grain for their starving families, Joseph revealed his identity to them and said, "You intended it for evil, but God intended it for good." Had Joseph not been sold into slavery, there would have been countless deaths, including those of his brothers and his father.

It's true. No one who does anything significant has done so without encountering a number of difficulties. Through the difficulties, God develops the character of the person that enables him to climb higher than he might have otherwise. God gives us great assurance, which Peter Marshall expressed quite well earlier in this commentary.

As a child of God with the mind of Christ and the fruit of the Holy Spirit and as a follower of the golden rule, I have an eternal Friend, and host of earthly friends, and marvelous family relationships. (Gal. 5:22; Matt. 7:12; 1 Cor 2:16)

God Doesn't Disagree with Himself

"GOD IS NOT telling you to go ahead if going ahead contradicts His Word."

Several years ago I met a young woman who was strongly committed to her faith. Later on she met a young man equally committed to his faith. They were married and, according to script, were supposed to have lived "happily ever after." However, she decided to quit her job and seek employment elsewhere. Because of her background and experience, she was able to find an excellent opportunity. A short time later she went to lunch with a man she met on her new job. Other lunches followed, even though her husband discouraged the practice. The inevitable took place: The two became more and more attached to each other, maintained they had fallen in love, and said they believed it was God's will that they had been brought together and that they should spend the rest of their lives together.

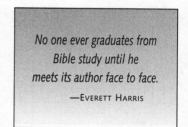

No one ever graduates from Bible study until he meets its author face to face.

—EVERETT HARRIS

With a straight face, she and her new love interest maintained that they had prayed about it, and it was in God's will. Regardless of their apparent sincerity, both of them, deep within their hearts, knew they were wrong. God never contradicts His Word, and when the divorce occurred, much grief was involved. Anytime people attempt to fit God's Word to their earthly will, they are in error, and grief and misery are the inevitable results.

God clearly tells us in Matthew 19 that He made both male and female, and that when a man marries, he leaves his father and mother and is to cling to his wife and they are to become one flesh. He tells us, "What God has joined together, let not man separate" (v. 6 NKJV). In Proverbs, we read Solomon's words that when a man finds a wife, he finds a good thing. The marriage vows themselves say that we are to "rejoice with the wife of our youth."

As a child of God, I guard my affections, for they influence everything else in my life. (Prov. 4:23)

Fan or Fanatic?

IF WE LOOK at the word *fanatic*, we discover that the first three letters spell *fan*. Most of us are fans of people, cities, companies, jobs, our mates, our faith, or the favorite athletic teams we support. I've always believed that loyal fans are real assets and that it helps to be a loyal fan.

However, a fanatic is something else. Eliminate *fan* from *fanatic*, and it becomes *atic*. I believe that people who become fanatics have an *atic* problem—in other words, they've taken it to an extreme and become so dogmatic that they endanger themselves or their careers. They lose the favorable influence they might have on other people, including their families.

It's one thing to believe in something or somebody. It's another thing to be completely blind to the fact that we can take it too far and that the person or team we favor might go too far in efforts to win. I believe that we can be loyal fans, supporting the activities that are productive, honorable, and solid, and calling into question the things that are illegal or immoral. For example, many of our "heroes" in the movies and on TV or in athletics have questionable personal lives.

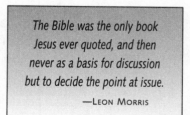

The Bible was the only book Jesus ever quoted, and then never as a basis for discussion but to decide the point at issue.
—LEON MORRIS

I believe it's fanaticism when you close your eyes to the bad and fanatically follow someone because "you've always been a fan."

Interestingly enough, when the individual, team, or politician realizes the negative behavior will not be tolerated any longer, chances are excellent that he or she will see the handwriting on the wall and make appropriate changes. I believe the real fan who is loyal but who holds the team or individual accountable for actions exercises responsibility.

In my childhood I observed a woman who was at every church function but seldom cooked a meal for her children. Their clothes were tattered and usually dirty. I would say that her judgment was clouded, to be kind to her. In reality, I would say that in her own way she was fanatical about being at church but used poor judgment and wasn't biblical in that she didn't take appropriate care of her children. Paul warned, "But if anyone does not provide for his own, and especially for those of his household, he has denied the faith and is worse than an unbeliever" (1 Tim. 5:8 NKJV).

I trust the Lord, so abiding love surrounds me. I rejoice in Him because I am His, and I shout for joy because I try to obey Him. (Ps. 32:10–11)

Friendly People

WHILE WE WERE in Tyler, Texas, my wife and I entered the Red Lobster restaurant and were pleasantly greeted by Tawanna, the young hostess who led us to a booth. Highlight number one. After a brief moment Stella, a transplant from New York who has been with Red Lobster for ten years, engaged the Redhead (my wife) in a pleasant and friendly conversation. Highlight number two. She told us Myra would be our waitperson, and in a matter of seconds Myra appeared. Stella had identified all of the wonderful specials for us. Myra pleasantly inquired if we were ready to order or if we wanted to order our drinks first. We both requested iced tea and

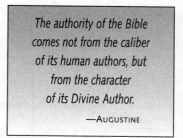

The authority of the Bible comes not from the caliber of its human authors, but from the character of its Divine Author.

—AUGUSTINE

water, and I asked Myra to bring me a cup of the clam chowder, explaining that when she returned, we would order our meals.

In only a few minutes Myra appeared with the chowder, took our order, and made her departure. The meal was delicious. Highlight number three.

We stopped by the grocery store on the way out of Tyler and had a pleasant interlude as we walked into the store. A young girl named Susie was walking out (her name was on her jacket), and I greeted her, "Susie, how are you?" She responded with the biggest smile I've ever seen, and it was obvious she thought she knew us and that we knew her. It was one of those little bright spots—highlight number four—that make all of us happy.

When you meet people, expect them to be nice, kind, and friendly. You increase your chances of meeting people like these by being nice, kind, friendly, and gracious yourself.

Christ said, "I was naked and you clothed Me; I was sick and you visited Me; I was in prison and you came to Me." He was asked, "When did we see You a stranger and take You in, or naked and clothe You? Or when did we see You sick, or in prison, and come to You?" And the King answered, "I say to you, inasmuch as you did it to one of the least of these My brethren, you did it to Me" (Matt. 25:36–40 NKJV).

I help the poor, so I am lending to the Lord [my responsibility] and He is paying me wonderful interest on the loan [His promise]. (Prov. 19:17)

Week Five

Beyond Closed Doors

BEYOND CLOSED DOORS is the title of a monthly publication "dedicated to inspiring the incarcerated to self-responsibility and motivating them to seek, find and develop that seed of greatness within themselves." The February 1998 issue carried a fascinating story that editor Kay P. Adkins titled "Success? You Decide."

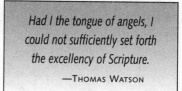

Had I the tongue of angels, I could not sufficiently set forth the excellency of Scripture.

—THOMAS WATSON

Think about the following story while you consider what success means to you. As two brothers entered their adult life, one completed college and became a highly successful lawyer while the other preferred the outdoors and traveled the country working as a park ranger, outdoor tour guide, seasonal crop worker, etc. The lawyer kept writing his vagabond brother to come live in the city, settle down, and pursue a "respectable" career. In an effort to persuade him, he would send his brother a picture of his BMW and write on the back, "My car," or a picture of his uptown condominium and write on the back, "My house," or a picture of his 40-story high-rise office building with "My office" written on the back. The other brother, finally tiring of the nonsense, put an end to the letters when he sent his lawyer brother a poster of the beautiful majestic Grand Teton Mountains in Wyoming. On the back of the poster he simply wrote, "My backyard."

Actually both men were successful. They just had different objectives for their lives.

I suspect that most of us, if we had the option, would prefer to follow the life of the brother who had that beautiful, majestic view in Wyoming. Message: You have lots of choices. As long as they're honorable, I encourage you to pursue those that fulfill your dreams because you will never be successful or happy pursuing someone else's dream.

God sends me peace and blesses me financially. (Ps. 147:14)

Yes—You Can Be Happy

ROSE BARTHEL SAID, "Happiness is a conscious choice. It is not an automatic response." Happiness is an attitude—not a *when* and a *where*, but a *here* and a *now*.

Dennis Prager said, "Fun is what we experience during an act. Happiness is what we experience after an act. It is a deeper, more abiding emotion." Going to an amusement park or ball game, or watching a movie or television program, helps us relax and temporarily forget our problems and maybe even laugh. But these activities do not bring happiness because their positive effect ends when the fun ends.

Prager also observed that people who claim to believe that a fun-filled, pain-free life equals happiness actually diminish their chances of attaining real happiness. If fun and pleasure equate with happiness, then it stands to reason that pain must equate with unhappiness. But the opposite is true. More times than not, things that lead to happiness involve some pain. He's right.

> In regard to this great book I have but to say it is the best gift God has given to men. All that the good Saviour gave to the world was communicated through this book.
>
> —ABRAHAM LINCOLN

Happiness is not pleasure; it's victory over odds that seem to be insurmountable.

For the last two decades Americans have pursued the almighty dollar, and our real purchasing power has gone up significantly. However, all studies indicate that the quality of life has not improved. In short, the pursuit of the money does not produce the happiness most people seek. Kids say they prefer their parents' presence over their presents. Husbands and wives say they want more time together, yet stay so busy either earning more money or watching television that time spent with friends and family has declined. By contrast, the Amish people, who are a religious, close-knit family group with few material goods, are much happier because they have the security of family and friends when difficulties come.

Cultivate friendships and stay close to your family because one of these days you will say either, "I'm glad I did," or "I wish I had."

––––––––––––––––––

When I am too weak to have any faith left, He remains faithful to me and will help me, for He cannot disown me; I am a part of Him, and He will always carry out His promises to me. (2 Tim. 2:13)

Choice—Laugh About It or Cry About It

I CHECKED INTO a Florida hotel at approximately 9:00 P.M. and noticed the light over the desk in my room wouldn't work. A new bulb didn't help, but since I had work to do, I figured I could adapt. Next I discovered the coffeemaker and the air conditioner wouldn't work. I wanted to watch Larry King interview Billy Graham, but the TV wasn't working either.

I called and asked for another room. The person at the desk countered that the maintenance man would "come right up and fix it," and within a couple of minutes he was there. He quickly discovered the need for another part and left to get it. After a delay I went to the desk and again asked for another room.

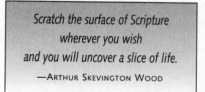

Scratch the surface of Scripture
wherever you wish
and you will uncover a slice of life.
—ARTHUR SKEVINGTON WOOD

Incidentally, everyone was courteous, pleasant, friendly, and agreeable. After another short wait someone called to say that I could have another room. I repacked my bags, and rather than await the offered assistance, I stopped by the desk and picked up the key. The key would not open the door to the new room, but the maintenance man reappeared and used his key to let me in, then turned on the TV set to show that it was working. I sat down to catch the interview, but the audio on Larry King's show was inaudible.

Did I laugh or cry? The challenges weren't life threatening. The bed looked comfortable; the shower, telephone, air-conditioning, and coffeemaker worked, so I just laughed.

The next day after a television appearance I returned to the hotel and saw this sign above the door: "This hotel has been acknowledged as one of the top twenty hotels in the world for this international organization."

I couldn't change the condition of the accommodations, so I chose to laugh and not get upset. I made the right choice. You can make positive choices when you understand that it's not what happens to you but how you handle what happens that will determine where you go in life.

———————————————————

I pray much for others and plead for God's mercy on them and give thanks for all He is going to do for them. (1 Tim. 2:1)

No Matter What

IN THE HIGHLY competitive world of college athletics, two things are critical: (1) the players recruited and (2) the coaches hired to direct their activities and mold a group of young individual stars into a team. One of the best in the business is football coach Bob Simmons, who is doing a great job at Oklahoma State University. During a recruiting season Bob offered Kenyana Tolbert a college scholarship and added the words, "We are committed to you, no matter what." Kenyana was a spectacular athlete, a star safety on defense, a wide receiver on offense, and a star on his high school basketball team.

When Tolbert visited the school to check out the team, the Oklahoma State Cowboys put on a splendid display. Tolbert liked everything he saw and told Coach Simmons he was committed to Oklahoma State.

> *The more reverence we have for the Word of God the more joy we shall find in it.*
> —MATTHEW HENRY

A few weeks later Kenyana Tolbert went down in a high school game with a critical injury. He dislocated two vertebrae in his back and couldn't move his limbs or breathe on his own. Tolbert entered a rehabilitation institute in Dallas and made progress, but he will never play football again. Nevertheless,

Simmons assured him that he meant what he said—Tolbert had the scholarship, "no matter what."

Since every scholarship is vital to the coach's winning, it was truly a class act built on character. What a role model this coach is to young players! He personifies integrity and considers his word his bond. I'm convinced that many parents will hear this story and decide that Coach Simmons would make an ideal coach for their son. Yes, I'm firmly convinced that the good guys really do win on the football field and in life.

God's love and kindness are better to me than life itself, and I praise and bless Him all my life. I lift up my hands in prayer and am fully satisfied as I praise Him with great joy. (Ps. 63:3–5)

Hugging at Home and at Work

AN ASSOCIATED PRESS article pointed out that hugging became corporate policy at Health Care & Retirement Corp. in Toledo, Ohio. The company sent every employee through an eleven-hour training program to make certain the hugging was appropriate, properly done, and not the result of one being physically attracted to a member of the opposite sex.

Psychologist Greg Risberg conducted the seminars and pointed out that hugs ranged from sympathetic embraces to celebratory "Gee, you did a great job!" hugs. However, he did not encourage anyone to find a person to whom he was attracted and give her a big hug. That last observation is particularly important in light of the sometimes fine line between being supportive and sexual harassment. That line is defined by the individual's perception about what is taking place. And we all know how widely perceptions can vary. Never risk unnecessary misunderstandings.

> Many books in my library are now behind and beneath me. They were good in their way once, and so were the clothes I wore when I was ten years old; but I have outgrown them. Nobody ever outgrows Scripture; the book widens and deepens with our years.
>
> —CHARLES H. SPURGEON

Hugging is important, and one final note for each husband who reads this: let me assure you that your wife resents it when you ignore her all day and then give her your undivided attention when the lights go out at night. She wants a hug when all you've got on your mind is a hug. Romance—real romance—takes place all over the house throughout the day and is not confined to the darkness of the bedroom. It has been stated that four hugs a day are required for survival and eight or ten hugs a day if life is really going to be lived. Fifteen or more will put you in high gear. Take the proper hugging approach to life, and life will be even more rewarding.

I trust You, Lord, and my thoughts often turn to you so I am in perfect peace. (Isa. 26:3)

Week Six

A Rainy Day Story

TODAY WAS ONE of those days. I don't believe I've ever seen so much rain fall so hard or so long. My wife and I were on our way to Tyler, Texas, to make some purchases, and to see Dr. John Hudnall, an ear, nose, and throat specialist, because I had a little physical problem. A blood vessel had apparently burst in my nose, and I had experienced some bleeding the past two nights.

When we arrived at Dr. Hudnall's office, we filled out the necessary forms and were ushered into an adjoining office. We listened as Dr. Hudnall talked with another patient. He was kind and gentle, and the tone of his voice indicated he was a doctor interested in the care of his patients. He treated me with the same courtesy, and he pointed out that he had every reason to believe he had spotted the culprit and cauterization would solve the problem. He finished the procedure

> The Bible as a revelation from God was not designed to give us all the information we might desire, nor to solve all the questions about which the human soul is perplexed, but to impart enough to be a safe guide to the haven of eternal rest.
>
> —ALBERT BARNES

53

and indicated he thought the problem was solved. He suggested I buy a nasal spray to use for a couple of days, and bid us a pleasant good-bye. He truly is an old-fashioned doctor practicing up-to-date medical care.

Christ, of course, is the Great Physician, who is kind, loving, gentle, and the ultimate in healing. Doctors cut and prescribe; Christ heals. Dr. Randolph Byrd, a board-certified cardiologist at San Francisco General Hospital, researched 393 patients who'd had heart attacks or severe chest pain. Half of them were prayed for at a distance from another city. The patients didn't know whether they were being prayed for or not. Among the group of patients being prayed for, there were fewer deaths, and they required less medication, such as antibiotics and diuretics. The people who were being prayed for did not require being intubated (having a tube placed down their throats) or hooked up to the mechanical breathing machine, while twelve people from the group that was not prayed for had to have these procedures. It was a statistically significant study, and there are many more similar ones to support the finding.

Message: Prayer works even if you are not aware that you are being prayed for.

I trust and reverence the Lord and have turned my back on evil [my responsibility], so He has given me renewed health and vitality [His promise]. (Prov. 3:7–8)

Laugh, Cry, or Do Something

WE'VE ALL USED the expression, "I didn't know whether to laugh or cry." To this, I will add a third option: do something about it.

According to Paul Craig Roberts, economist with the Cato Institute, the Washington, D.C., Rescue Service has an employee who is a carrier of hepatitis B, an infectious disease. The department keeps him on but told him not to perform mouth-to-mouth resuscitation. He filed a discrimination lawsuit, and Federal District Judge Joyce Green ruled that "public health be damned, the worker was covered under the Americans With Disabilities Act and the D.C. government could not prevent the infected worker from giving mouth-to-mouth resuscitation."

> God's Word is like a log sitting on top of the ice on a frozen lake. When the ice thaws and melts, the log penetrates into the water and becomes a part of the lake. The trials that come along in life are like that thawing process. They melt the heart and allow God's Word to penetrate and become a part of us.

The Justice Department gave Aurora, Illinois, a surprise Christmas present one year—a lawsuit. It so happens that Aurora doesn't have any police officers using wheelchairs or any firefighters with chronic back problems, so the city was slapped with a lawsuit for discriminating against disabled persons.

In Jefferson City, Missouri, a five-pound, one-thousand-page bill became law without the governor's signature. Its goal: to reduce state paperwork. This helps to explain why Eugene McCarthy was moved to say, "The only thing that saves us from bureaucracy is its inefficiency." A new poll highlighted the truth of his words: 58 percent of Americans feel the government is too big; the government is the remaining 42 percent. This also helps to explain why many politicians are unhappy because they are underpaid, underappreciated, and under investigation.

Don't misunderstand. I'm opposed to discrimination, but I'm convinced common sense is more important for the common good. We need to work hard to make our laws fair and practical.

I can say without any doubt or fear that the Lord is my helper and I am not afraid of anything that mere man can do to me. (Heb. 13:6)

Sensitivity Can Make a Huge Difference

A GENTLEMAN I know quite well had an interesting experience. His wife was recuperating at home from surgery and maintaining a light schedule. She could move about, but getting up and down and bending were particularly painful. A couple of days after she came home from the hospital, he was up early in the morning and went downstairs for a cup of coffee. His favorite cup was in the dishwasher, and as he retrieved it, he noticed that the dishwasher was full of clean dishes. Remembering that his wife was recuperating, he unloaded the dishwasher. It took only five minutes to complete the job.

After finishing his coffee, he went back to the bedroom to get ready for work and left before his wife went to the kitchen. That evening when he returned home, she gave him a big hug and thanked him profusely for what he had done. She said, "Honey, I cried when I realized I would not have to bend over all of those times and lift those dishes out." He had made a simple gesture, but it spoke volumes to

> The Bible is to us what the star was to the wise men; but if we spend all our time in gazing upon it, observing its motions, and admiring its splendor, without being led to Christ by it, the use of it will be lost to us.
>
> —THOMAS ADAMS

his wife. It indicated that he genuinely cared for her, her comfort, and her well-being. It was not monumental, but isn't it true that the little things make the big difference in life?

Think about it. If your watch is slow by just four minutes, that's not much—unless you've been warned that being even one minute late ever again will get you fired. Then four minutes become important.

Be sensitive to the needs of others and remember the little things in life because they make big differences—especially if you make those little things a way of life.

In response to all He has done for me I go overboard in being help-ful and kind to others and doing good. (Heb. 10:24)

It Ain't Funny

WHEN I WAS a youngster, movies often depicted drunken people as being hilariously funny. All too often—then and now—drinking alcohol is depicted as a humorous and harmless social habit to acquire.

Unfortunately, the public presentations of alcohol, particularly in the beer and wine commercials, lead us to believe that drinking truly brings about "the good life." However, every health authority understands there is a downside to making alcohol appear glamorous and attractive. Maggie Fox, health and science correspondent for a newspaper, observes that children who start drinking before age fifteen are four times more likely to become alcoholics, formally known as "alcohol dependent," as people who start at age twenty-one. Forest Tennant, M.D., says that the younger a person starts drinking, the more likely he is to develop serious drinking problems. The idea that we should teach our children to

> In this one book are the two most interesting personalities in the whole world—God and yourself. The Bible is the story of God and man, a love story in which you and I must write our own ending, our unfinished autobiography of the creature and the Creator.
>
> —FULTON OURSLER

drink is absurd. How much better it would be to teach them *not* to drink!

A thirteen-year-old who starts drinking has more than a 25 percent chance of becoming an alcoholic—and if there is a family history of alcohol abuse, that percentage is 58 percent. Research indicates that if young people wait until twenty-one to start drinking, only 10 percent develop a drinking problem. However, "only 10 percent" means that 10 percent of our young people end up in the alcoholic jungle, and that percentage takes on an entirely different meaning—especially if your son or daughter or someone else you care about is in that 10 percent.

There are many drawbacks to alcohol consumption, including risky sexual activity, which leads to unwanted pregnancy, exposure to the HIV virus, and other sexually transmitted diseases. Alcohol is also strongly linked to violence, depression, and suicide.

Copy this information and stick it on the bathroom mirror so your young people can read it as they get old enough to read. Who knows? Perhaps it will save your family from tragedy.

To young men, I am a good example of good deeds of every kind, and everything I do reflects my love of the truth and the fact that I am earnest about it. (Titus 2:6–7)

Leadership with Integrity

IT IS TRUE that integrity alone won't make you a leader, but without integrity you will never be one. A classic example involving integrity is one displayed by Steuben, the manufacturer of crystal. For generations the firm has had a policy of breaking every imperfect piece of crystal, no matter how small the flaw. Needless to say, this is a potent symbolic act to both employees and customers. By the same token, genuine leaders must resolve to uphold their standards and values and act as role models for everyone in the organization. If leaders don't place values on a pedestal and defend them against attack, who will?

A person of integrity will make many decisions in advance.

> It is a fortress often attacked but never failing.
> Its wisdom is commanding and its logic convincing.
> Salvation is its watchword. Eternal life its goal.
> It punctures all pretense.
> It is forward-looking, outward-looking, and upward-looking.
> It outlives, outlifts, outloves, outreaches, outranks, outruns all other books.
> Trust it, love it, obey it, and Eternal Life is yours.
>
> —A. Z. CONRAD

He is guided by principles, and he makes decisions not for each individual situation, but according to principle. When values are well established within an organization, the integrity principle will lead to decisions of integrity as those countless occasions arise where there has been no specific prior example. In this way the organization avoids serious pitfalls.

Leaders with integrity know they are not infallible. When they make the inevitable mistakes, they acknowledge their errors and immediately make amends. In other words, they are big enough to admit their shortcomings and wise enough to right their wrongs as quickly as possible.

In his books and speeches, former Notre Dame head football coach Lou Holtz regularly admonishes people to "do the right thing." When you do the right thing, even if the results are not good, your integrity remains intact; your followers' confidence in you is not irreparably damaged because they know you are a person of integrity.

I listen to God and do what He tells me, so I will have a long, good life. (Prov. 4:10 NLT)

Week Seven

A Cup of Yogurt

WHEN I WAS in Sacramento, California, I had an hour's delay before my flight left. I walked over to the yogurt stand and ordered my favorite concoction, a mixture of the white chocolate mousse and fresh strawberries. As the woman was preparing it, I was impressed with her thoroughness. She presented me with yogurt that was completely blended and absolutely delicious.

After I finished my yogurt, I engaged the woman in conversation. She was of Oriental descent, from Taiwan, and had been in America for seventeen years. I asked her how long it had taken her to get a job when she came to America. She said, "One day," with a big smile. Then I commented that she was certainly pleasant, enthusiastic, and very capable at what she was doing. She handed me her business card, on which was printed "David and Kelly Tu." This business card, as she proudly explained, gave the location for their restaurant, Tu's Hunan Restaurant.

> It is a miracle how God has so long preserved this Book, how great and glorious it is to have the Word of God.
>
> —MARTIN LUTHER

Following a short, pleasant conversation with her, I started contemplating the fact that in 1981, when Kelly Tu arrived in America, our economy was not robust. Yet she had gone to work the first day. Now she and her husband have a restaurant. I have no idea how they are doing, but if her husband has anything approaching her spirit and attitude, they're doing quite well. Kelly Tu is a happy individual, enjoying what she is doing and grateful for her opportunities in America.

As I think on these things, I wonder what would happen if more people adopted this young woman's attitude, went to work, smiled about what they were doing, and gave it their best shot? I have an idea they would do well.

In plain language, the Bible says a lot about work and attitude: "While we were with you, we gave you this rule: 'Whoever does not work should not eat'" (2 Thess. 3:10 NLT); and "Work hard and cheerfully at whatever you do" (Col. 3:23 NLT).

Work on earth produces earthly rewards. But John 6:29 (NKJV) tells us about heavenly rewards: "Jesus answered and said to them, 'This is the work of God, that you believe in Him whom He sent.'" In short, you believe your way to heaven; you don't work your way there.

I thank You, Father, for giving me rest from my hard work and heavy yoke. (Matt. 11:28)

You Transfer Your Feelings

FOR YEARS I have believed and taught that selling is simply a transference of feeling, and in life everything is a feeling. The salesperson transfers feeling when he makes the prospect feel the same way he does about the product he is selling, and the prospect frequently buys. When a leader has a passion for the mission of the company and verbalizes as well as lives that passion, the employees first pick up the feeling, which springs their minds open. Then they buy into the concepts.

Ray Charles is a classic example of this concept. His mother told him when he was a youngster, "Be yourself, son," and Ray Charles has always followed that advice. The fact that his career spans fifty years says something about the validity of the concept. Charles says, "I like songs that tell me a story, that make me feel something. That way I can make other people feel what I feel." He must be successful because he has received several Grammy Awards and other awards for his work.

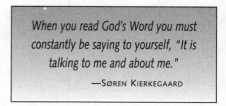

When you read God's Word you must constantly be saying to yourself, "It is talking to me and about me."
—SØREN KIERKEGAARD

David Ritz, who cowrote *Brother Ray: Ray Charles' Own Story,* says, "It doesn't matter whether he's singing the blues or

R&B or country or jazz. The power of his personality overwhelms the genre he's singing. He has no respect for categories. He's just as happy to do a George Jones tune as he is to do a Percy Mayfield tune."

Ray always tells songwriters, "Don't try to write a Ray Charles song, just give me a good song and I'll make it a Ray Charles song." "Everything he touches is like that," adds longtime friend Quincy Jones.

If you believe in what you feel and in what you're doing, and you have a passion for it, you can communicate that to other people, and success is inevitably the result.

I rest in the Lord and wait patiently for Him to act. I trust Him and humble myself before Him [my responsibility]. I am given every blessing and have wonderful peace [God's promise]. (Ps. 37:7–11)

The Way We Reveal Ourselves

THERE'S AN OLD adage that says who you are speaks much louder than what you say. That old saying holds much truth, but reality tells us that we reveal ourselves in many ways: the company we keep, the way we use our free time, the clothing we wear, the things that appeal to our sense of humor, the way we talk, and the way we handle our successes as well as our failures. It's also safe to say that we reveal ourselves by the way we deal with people who are less fortunate mentally, physically, financially, or socially. The smile or frown, the look of compassion or anger, reveals much of who we are and what we believe. In short, we are walking encyclopedias about ourselves.

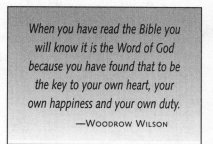

When you have read the Bible you will know it is the Word of God because you have found that to be the key to your own heart, your own happiness and your own duty.
—WOODROW WILSON

However, once we become aware that everything we do is a showcase of who we are, we can make necessary changes and begin to work toward becoming more other-person-centered and less self-centered.

The brief words of C. S. Lewis speak volumes: "If you live for the next world, you get this one in the deal. But if you live only for this world, you lose them both." Whether we live for this world or the next world is revealed through our treatment of others; our beliefs; our conduct in our personal, family, and business lives; and our care and concern for friends, relatives, neighbors, and associates. As Margaret Thatcher wisely observed, "The Good Samaritan story would never have been told had he not stopped to render aid." All of us have the potential to be a good Samaritan by the care we feel and give to others.

Stephen Arterburn put it this way: "Win small before you try to win big; commit to excellence in whatever you do; and, at the same time, commit to service. Those who succeed in order to serve find fulfillment and meaning that others who seek only power will never have." In short, he's saying we need to think about others as the good Samaritan did, and that way we will enjoy a better life here and an eternal life that will be beyond comprehension.

Earthly Benefits:
I put God first in everything I do [my responsibility]. He directs me and crowns my effort with success [God's promise]. (Prov. 3:6)

Heavenly Blessings:
I have confessed with my mouth that Jesus is Lord and believe in my heart that God raised Him from death [my responsibility]. I will be saved [God's promise]. (Rom. 10:9)

Never Too Old

GEORGE DAWSON was born on January 18, 1898. He was just eight years old when he had his first job and twelve when "his daddy rented him out to a white man." His brothers and sisters learned to read at a school "for colored children." George didn't get to go to school because he was the oldest child and had to work. He married in 1926 and was a father in 1927. He held a variety of odd jobs including chopping wood, working in a sawmill, and building levees. He laid ties for the railroad in east Texas, swept floors, cleaned houses, and for most of his working life ran machines that pasteurized milk at Oak Farms Dairy.

George got by without reading for ninety-eight years and simply trusted people who paid his wages and his wife who read the bills. In 1996 at age ninety-eight, George Dawson decided he was tired of fishing and it was time to read. When his teacher started him with six letters, he interrupted him and said, "No, son, I want to see all of them so

> *The Word of God, well understood and religiously obeyed, is the shortest route to spiritual perfection. And we must not select a few favorite passages to the exclusion of others. Nothing less than a whole Bible can make a whole Christian.*
>
> —A. W. TOZER

I can put them together." He learned his ABCs in just a day and a half and moved on to phonics, breaking the words into pieces and sounding out the parts. He impatiently said, "No, son, I want to say something that makes sense." For four hours every day, Monday through Friday, the determined man sat in the same seat on the second row.

At the end of the first month he could write his name, and after almost two years, he could read at a third-grade level. He read the Scriptures aloud at Holiness Church of God if they asked him. He's now over one hundred, but he's still excited about life and still learning.

You eighty- or ninety-year-old "kids," take a lesson from George Dawson: keep learning, and you'll live longer and have more fun on the trip. Not only that, but psychiatrist Smiley Blanton says he has never met a senile person, regardless of age, who did three things: (1) stayed active physically, (2) continued to grow mentally, and (3) developed a genuine interest in other people. Doing these things will enable you to maintain your mental capabilities, regardless of age. Psychiatrist Frank Minirth agrees with the observation that Alzheimer's is a disease, but senility, in most cases, is the result of a long series of poor choices. Choose to read, learn, and grow, and your life will truly be richer and more rewarding.

I will do whatever it takes to be one who lives in the fresh newness of life of those who are alive from the dead. (Phil. 3:11)

Public Speaking Tips

ACCORDING TO *Reader's Digest*, public speaking is the number one fear in America, so here are some tips that will relieve you of some of your anxiety.

First, as far as I know, Barbara Helleen, who suffered a fatal heart attack while speaking to the Women's Club of Rosendale, New York; Alben W. Barkley, former vice president of the United States; and Arthur MacArthur, father of Douglas MacArthur, are the only people to have died while making a speech. There have been literally billions of speeches made, yet few fatalities while doing so. Message: It's safe to make a speech!

Second, remember that if you took an old Georgia mule—or, for that matter, a Tennessee or Florida one—and led him across the stage in front of thousands of people, he would almost go to sleep on the trip. However, if you took a thoroughbred racehorse across that same stage, he would be

> I must confess to you that the majesty of the Scriptures astonishes me. The holiness of the evangelist speaks to my heart and has such striking character of truth and is, moreover, so perfectly inimitable that if it had been the invention of men, the inventors would be greater than the greatest heroes.
>
> —JEAN-JACQUES ROUSSEAU

jumping all over the place. Message: If you get a little nervous before you speak, just be grateful you're a thoroughbred and not a mule.

Third, don't try to impress the skeptics, or the sourpusses. As you speak, whether in front of ten or ten thousand, pick out a smiling face and talk directly to that person. Every few seconds shift your eyes to another "smiler." Do this throughout your talk and the sourpusses will probably come around, but regardless don't let them discourage you or affect your attitude.

Final tip: Localize your talk to make it applicable to your audience or your situation. These thoughts will help you to survive, and with practice even thrive!

Pubic speaking has many benefits. It builds confidence, and the general public believes that those who can stand up and make sense on their feet have an intelligence that is way above average. Obviously that's not necessarily true, but perception is important, so learning to speak could help you in your personal, family, and business lives.

I have no fear, even if the world blows up and the mountains crumble into the sea, because I am filled with the river of joy that flows through the city of God, where God Himself lives. (Ps. 46:2–5)

Week Eight

What Good Does It Do?

WORRY IS nothing new among the human race, but it escalated substantially as we approached the year 2000. As it turned out, Y2K was much ado about nothing. We not only survived, but also, with the exception of a few fear-induced glitches, things were normal.

Various people have described worry as "interest paid on trouble before it comes due" and "stewing without doing." An article in *Psychology Today* indicated that writing down what we

---

On the cover of your Bible and my Bible appear the words, "Holy Bible." Do you know why the Bible is called holy? Why should it be called holy when so much lust and hate and greed and war are found in it? I can tell you why. It is because the Bible tells the truth. It tells the truth about God, about man, and about the devil. The Bible teaches that we exchange the truth of God for the devil's lie. About sex, for example, and drugs and alcohol and religious hypocrisy. Jesus Christ is the ultimate truth. Furthermore, He told the truth. Jesus said that He was the Truth, and the Truth would make us free.

—BILLY GRAHAM

---

are worrying about puts it in the proper perspective and often eliminates the worry.

After writing your concerns, ask yourself, Why am I concerned about this? Is there anything I can do about it? Does it affect me directly or even indirectly? For example, Should I really be concerned that a friend of mine has a next-door neighbor who plays loud music late at night and disturbs his sleep? It's fine to express interest in and empathize with your friend's concern, but worrying about it is truly a waste of your best resource—namely, your creative mind.

If the concern is legitimate, then you must ask yourself, Specifically what can I do about it? What is my plan of action? The moment you begin to consider solutions to solve the problem, you feel better because action always creates an emotion that is healthier and more conducive to success than just worrying about it. Research at UCLA validates that people who have a plan of action to accomplish specific objectives (such as overcoming worry) are happier as a result. Take this approach, and you'll be a happier, healthier you as you go about your daily life.

God has worked out His plans for my life and His loving-kindness continues forever. He won't abandon me, for He made me. (Ps. 138:8)

Just Nice Folks

ON DECEMBER 30, 1997, the weather gave us a gorgeous day, but we had a slight plumbing problem. We don't visit our home at Holly Lake very often, and the cold water knob in the master bedroom shower wouldn't budge, making it very difficult to turn on the water. My daughter Cindy Oates and her husband, Richard, were spending the week with us, and Richard is a builder/plumber/jack-of-all-trades. He volunteered to fix the shower.

> The Bible is God's chart for you to steer by, to keep you from the bottom of the sea, and to show you where the harbor is and how to reach it without running on rocks or bars.
>
> —HENRY WARD BEECHER

We drove into Tyler, Texas, and went to three locations trying to find replacement parts with no luck. Someone at our third stop told us about a veteran of many plumbing wars at Hamilton's Plumbing Supply. He showed immediate interest and indicated he thought he could handle the dilemma. He put the errant part into a vise, and with two other men went to work on it. The men spent quite some time putting it back into working order.

The entire operation took more than an hour. What did it cost me? Nearly seven dollars—and that was for the replacement parts.

Please understand. We live in Dallas, 110 miles away, yet they treated us like long-lost cousins. They would have been better off financially had we never darkened their door. Why did they do it? They're just nice folks.

In our high-pressure, hurry-hurry-hurry, hooray-for-me world, these men at Hamilton's Plumbing enjoy what they do and are willing to serve. I hope the folks in Tyler, Texas, will read these words and decide to do business with them. If they do, I'll bet they'll be glad they did!

They understand the benefits of good service. Albert Schweitzer said, "I don't know what your destiny will be, but one thing I know—the only ones among you who will be really happy are those who have sought and found how to serve." Henry Miller commented, "Render a service if you would succeed. This is the supreme law of life. Be among the great servers, the benefactors. It is the only path to success. 'Give and it shall be given unto you.' Make society your debtor and you may find your place among the immortals."

I do not get tired of doing what is right, so after a while I will reap a harvest of blessing, and that's why I'll always try to be kind to everyone, especially my Christian brothers. (Gal. 6:9–10)

The Price Is Right

IN THE DAYS of yesteryear a Chinese rice farmer was working at his hilltop farm. He saw the ocean swiftly withdraw from the shore, much like a huge animal crouching just before it pounces on its prey. He instinctively knew that a huge tidal wave would quickly follow. Seeing his neighbors working in their fields by the seashore and knowing their only means of escape was to run to the hills, he set fire to his rice field and then furiously rang the temple bell as a warning to them.

> God has favored us with His autobiography so that we might know and think His thoughts in every department of our lives.
> —ROBERT HORN

From the seashore his neighbors saw the fire and rushed to help him. From the safety of his hilltop, they watched the water as it swirled over the fields they had just left. They knew their safety had been bought at a price.

Do we ever reflect on what has been bought for us at a price? Our freedom was bought at a price. Lincoln paid for the freeing of the slaves with his life. Many of us enjoy things today that were bought at a price.

Some of the best-educated people in America today got that way because from the time they were born, their parents set aside money on a regular basis to pay for their education. Many of us enjoy good health because scientists have spent time in laboratories researching and finding drugs and medicines that improve our health.

The list is endless. But do we ever take time to write a note, make a phone call, or otherwise express appreciation to those who bought our pleasures and luxuries with their own sacrifice? You would be amazed at the response you will get if you do. The recipient of your compliment will be delighted, and you will feel even better than the recipient does.

Something as simple as a smile can bring amazing results. When you smile at someone, he spontaneously smiles back. Even people who might have frowns on their faces, who are desperately in need of a smile, will usually return yours. They'll feel better because of their own smile, which came as a result of your smiling at them. You'll feel better in the process. As the old saying goes, "A smile is a little curve that sets a lot of things straight." Give it a try, and you'll be glad you did.

I don't use bad language. I say only what is good and helpful to those I am talking to, and I give them a blessing in the process. (Eph. 4:29)

Dennis the Menace

I'LL CONFESS that Dennis the Menace is my favorite philosopher. Of all the comic strip characters, Dennis fills a need in my life—namely, to be forced to think and to be encouraged to laugh.

Some time ago a Dennis cartoon portrayed what many people would describe as a vivid picture of grace that, biblically speaking, is "the unmerited favor of God." Dennis was walking away from the Wilsons' house with his friend and sidekick, Joey. Both boys had their hands full of cookies, and Joey asked, "I wonder what we did to deserve this?" Dennis delivered the answer packed with truth: "Look, Joey, Mrs. Wilson gives us cookies not because we're nice, but because she's nice."

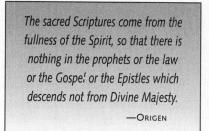

The sacred Scriptures come from the fullness of the Spirit, so that there is nothing in the prophets or the law or the Gospel or the Epistles which descends not from Divine Majesty.

—ORIGEN

A writer whose article was published in the *Houston Chronicle* on July 13, 1995, pointed out that "with the quick pen of an editor, my name could be replaced for Dennis and Mrs. Wilson could be replaced by God. The good which comes my way is not because I am good, but because God is good."

We can take this one more step and say that many times we

are the recipients of kindness and gifts of significance not because we're good, but because the giver is good, kind, and generous. The interesting twist to all of this is that the more kind and generous we are to others, the more people there are who will be kind and generous to us. Take to heart what Dennis is teaching us in this simple little cartoon, and you'll end up with more of the good things of life as well as more pleasure and happiness. Most of us would call that a good deal.

In reality, I'm talking about practicing the golden rule—treat other people as you want to be treated. Think about how rich and happy your life would be if everybody you met would go out of his way to treat you exactly as he wants to be treated! Now reverse the thought, and treat everyone as you want to be treated. Other people will receive incredible joy and happiness from it—but not as much as you will!

I serve the Lord with reverent fear and I rejoice with trembling, and oh, what joy that is because I put my trust in Him. (Ps. 2:11–12)

The Integrity Approach

FORTUNATELY, PEOPLE are demanding that we return to ethical standards. It's a buzzword in our society, and it's about time. Unfortunately they're using the wrong word. We should be concerned about teaching *integrity,* because people with integrity will behave in an ethical manner.

In *Faith Fax Daily Devotions,* Dr. Jay Strack wrote that "integrity involves realistic harmony of our talk and our walk. Integrity shines in the congruity of our behavior with our belief." In his book *Integrity,* Dr. Stephen Carter noted that it is "summarized as 'true virtue' with a sense of uprightness, honesty and sincerity. The *Oxford English Dictionary* includes three ideas: 'wholeness, perfection and uprightness.' Our colloquial expression is that people of integrity 'have it all together.'

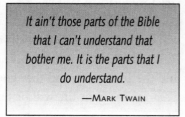

It ain't those parts of the Bible that I can't understand that bother me. It is the parts that I do understand.

—MARK TWAIN

"Integrity is the lack of pretense," continued Dr. Strack.

> In contrast to the image-polishing hype of a marketing-oriented world, it is the simple innocence of being one's transformed self without regard to the opinions or judgment of a godless society.

Two word pictures of sincerity are instructive to the meaning of integrity. Our word "sincere" actually is derived from two Latin words, *sine* and *cere,* which mean "without" and "wax." In making furniture, wax was used to fill in pitchpockets and to conceal mars in the wood or mistakes of the carpenter. Skillfully treated with wax, the blemish was covered, looking well for sale but later hard usage or heat brought out the wax cover-up. A merchant of integrity would write on his products *sine cere* (without wax), guaranteeing genuineness.

Grenville Kleiser discussed integrity in this way: "You are already of consequence in the world if you are known as a man of strict integrity, if you can be absolutely relied upon. If when you say a thing is so it is so, if when you say you will do a thing you will do it, then you carry with you a passport to universal esteem."

Live and act with integrity, and you will have genuine success and the peace of mind that goes with having a clear conscience. That means your life will be far less complicated.

I stand before the Lord with pure hands and heart and do not practice dishonesty or lying, so I receive God's goodness as my blessing from Him because He planted it in me. (Ps. 24:4–5)

Week Nine

Just Add a Zero

BEN FELDMAN is arguably the greatest life insurance salesperson of all time. In his career he sold more insurance than some companies do; however, he struggled to get started and had difficulty selling a $5,000 policy. Over the years, he started thinking that if instead of a $5,000 policy he could just add one zero to it, it would take him no more time, he could render far more service, and everyone would win. He pursued that idea and raised his sights. Sure enough, in a reasonably short period of time he was selling $50,000 insurance policies.

> The faith will totter if the authority of the Holy Scriptures loses its hold on men. We must surrender ourselves to the authority of Holy Scripture, for it can neither mislead nor be misled.
>
> —AUGUSTINE

As he pondered this situation one day, he asked himself if he dared add one more zero and sell $500,000 policies. Sure enough, the early success increased his confidence. He moved his sales up another zero, and $500,000 policies came with regularity.

You've probably guessed the next step, and you're right. He added another zero, and soon he was selling $5 million policies. Incredibly enough, one day he enlarged it by adding another zero and started selling $50 million life insurance policies.

Yes, I'll admit it's an incredible story, especially for such a shy man. When the life underwriters invited him to speak at their national meeting, he asked for a large screen so that he could stand behind it to make his talk. Ben Feldman, the greatest life insurance salesman of all time, was intimidated by that crowd. Incidentally, he did the bulk of his business in and near the small town of New Liverpool, Ohio.

Achieving a small goal increases your confidence, and you will raise your sights. Who knows? Maybe we all need to add more zeros (small steps) to our lives.

It took a lot of courage and imagination for Ben Feldman to keep moving his objectives higher and higher until they reached astronomical heights. You might think his achievement is so incredible that you could never do anything like that. The truth is that "eternal arithmetic" teaches that you plus God equals doing some mighty things. In 1 Corinthians 2:9 (NLT) we read, "No eye has seen, no ear has heard, and no mind has imagined what God has prepared for those who love him." Isaiah put it this way: "For since the world began, no ear has heard, and no eye has seen a God like you, who works for those who wait for him!" (Isa. 64:4 NLT).

My God-given wisdom gives me a long, good life, riches, honor, pleasure, and peace. (Prov. 3:16–17)

You Said It

WE REVEAL OURSELVES in many ways: by the people with whom we associate, our use of free time, our clothing, our sense of humor, and so forth. We reveal ourselves by the way we walk, the way we talk, the way we handle our successes and our failures. We reveal ourselves by the way we deal with people who are less fortunate physically, mentally, financially, and socially than we are, and by the way we talk to people we believe have more of all of the above than we have. The smile or frown, the look of compassion or anger, gives away our inner selves. In short, we are walking encyclopedias about ourselves, whether we speak or not. Yes, our actions reveal a great deal.

> The Bible appears like a symphony orchestra, with the Holy Ghost as its Toscanini. Each instrument has been brought willingly, spontaneously, creatively to play his notes, just as the great conductor desired, though none of them could ever hear the music as a whole.
>
> —J. I. PACKER

Too many of us permit our mouths to overload our backs, and we feel pressed too much of the time. Stephen Arterburn offered this advice: "Don't allow yourself to reach for more than you can handle. Win small before you try to win big. Commit to excellence whatever you do. In addition to excellence, commit to service. Those who succeed in order to serve find fulfillment and meaning that others who seek only power will never have." In short, he's saying to think about the other person.

Many years ago, William Penn said, "I expect to pass through life but once. If, therefore, there be any kindness I can show, or any good thing I can do to any fellow being, let me do it now and not defer or neglect it, as I shall not pass this way again." Henry Ward Beecher put it this way: "Though the world needs reproof and correction, it needs kindness more. Though it needs the grasp of the strong hand, it needs too the open palm of love and tenderness." My all-time favorite quote is this: "You can have everything in life you want if you will just help enough other people get what they want."

I do not quarrel with fellow Christians. I warn those who are lazy, comfort those who are frightened, take tender care of those who are weak, and am patient with everyone. (1 Thess. 5:13–14)

Rejection Produces Creativity

KATY GUEST applied for admission to the University of Missouri–Kansas City School of Dentistry, but the answer was no. She confessed to shedding a few tears and being discouraged when she got the rejection slip. Then her friend Guy and her parents thought she had given up and were upset with her. That, as she put it, "kicked me into shape." She decided she had two weeks to prove to the admissions committee that she had all the "right stuff" to be a qualified candidate.

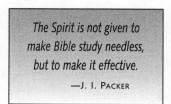

The Spirit is not given to make Bible study needless, but to make it effective.

—J. I. PACKER

She recalled what she had learned in a seminar given by Steve Anderson and Walter Hailey, and put it into practice.

> I wrote 10 letters in all, on different topics such as continuing ed, community service, update on my semester, etc., to the Committee. And in each letter I stood out from the pack by attaching a toothbrush, toothpaste, or floss with a catch slogan like:
>
> "I want to 'BRUSH AWAY' any doubt your committee might have . . ." "This is my 'FLOSSophy' about why I

would be a good candidate for your school." "I want to 'PASTE' my name in your minds . . ."

Anyway, the lady who called to inform me of my admission told me that I "wore them down" (ha, ha, ha). She said that never, in all her years of working at the dental school, had she ever seen anything like that done. I was very proud of myself for not giving up when the chips were down, and for persisting and being determined. Truly, persistence is an important key to success.

And so is your attitude. A cross-country truck driver always seemed relaxed and rested. A friend asked him why. The driver explained that he didn't go to work and take cross-country trips—he simply went for a ride in the country. Attitude makes a difference.

Katy demonstrated a considerable amount of creativity, but she also demonstrated a lot of character. There's always a risk when you persist as she did, but she had absolutely nothing to lose. They had already said no, so she took the risk. As the old saying goes, "Those who won't take a chance don't have a chance."

———————————

The Lord is directing my steps, so I don't try to understand everything that happens along the way. (Prov. 20:24)

Easy Street

MANY OF US have been looking for Easy Street all of our lives. But what happens when we get on Easy Street?

Bits and Pieces, a fascinating little magazine, gives us the answer in the form of some Hawaiian wisdom from the island of Oahu. If you take the Pali Highway northbound out of Honolulu, you will come to Pali Pass. At Pali Pass you can turn right on Park Street, go one block, and you will arrive at Easy Street. Turn left on Easy Street and drive one block; you will then see a sign that reads "Dead End."

The article concluded, "Those looking for the easy street of life are usually surprised by the road's predictable destination." To this, I would add that life has its ups and downs, and it really is tough. However, when we are tough on ourselves, life is infinitely easier on us. In short, everything is not going to be easy. Many things are going to be difficult, but we arrive on a much easier street by overcoming difficulties.

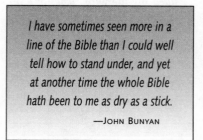

I have sometimes seen more in a line of the Bible than I could well tell how to stand under, and yet at another time the whole Bible hath been to me as dry as a stick.

—JOHN BUNYAN

As a salesman and as a sales trainer, I frequently have made the observation that the toughies are the teachers. When we encounter a prospect ready to buy, it's fun to write the order, but we don't learn anything from the transaction. When we meet a legitimate prospect who has lots of objections and gives us many reasons why he should not buy, and we effectively deal with him, we learn something about how to make other sales, which brings us even more success.

We read in Matthew 7:13–14 (NLT): "You can enter God's Kingdom only through the narrow gate. The highway to hell is broad, and its gate is wide for the many who choose the easy way. But the gateway to life is small, and the road is narrow, and only a few ever find it." The good news is that for those who do find it, God's promises are magnificent.

I honor the Lord by giving Him the firstfruits of my labor, so He has filled my life with riches and an abundance of the good things of life. (Prov. 3:9–10)

The Wind Has to Blow

VERY FEW PEOPLE go around asking for trouble. We certainly don't ask God to give us problems since life's so easy and we need a challenge. However, maybe we should.

Once I received an interesting note from Thomas Wylie of Westminster, Maryland. He wrote that he and his wife were visiting relatives in Tucson, Arizona, and while they were there they decided to visit the nearby Biosphere Two. The Biosphere Two was a man-made living habitat experiment. During the tour the guide explained that one oversight of the designers was their failure to create wind within the structure. No wind to blow the trees back and forth created a problem. The trees would grow to a certain height and then topple over from their own weight. Lack of wind resulted in the trees not having a deeply extended root system.

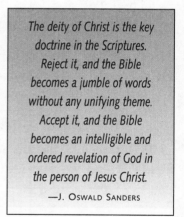

The deity of Christ is the key doctrine in the Scriptures. Reject it, and the Bible becomes a jumble of words without any unifying theme. Accept it, and the Bible becomes an intelligible and ordered revelation of God in the person of Jesus Christ.

—J. OSWALD SANDERS

Wylie then stated that this thought made him realize that without the winds of adversity, we cannot grow and become the people God designed us to be without toppling over. I agree. You cannot raise champions on a feather bed. The percentage of people who overcome adversity to go to great heights is legendary. Adversity develops character.

In the later years of her life my mother lamented that all of her children had been required to go to work at an early age. However, not one of my brothers or sisters regretted having to do so. We believed it gave us a jump start on life, and all of us believed that parents who do not teach their children responsibility end up with far more troubled kids than those who require them to do some of the tough things so they can enjoy more of the good things later in life.

From time to time when the weather doesn't suit us, all of us are inclined to say that we wish we could make it rain or stop raining, that the wind would blow more or less, that it would get cooler or warmer. The biosphere demonstrates to us that man is far more likely to forget some things or doesn't have the wisdom to know things, as he forgot to let the wind blow to encourage the trees to develop roots. We should be grateful that God is in control of the total picture, and although we might not understand His head, we can trust His heart.

I please God, so He gives me wisdom, knowledge, and joy. (Eccl. 2:26)

Week Ten

It's Smart to Be Nice

DEFINING *nice* presents a challenge. However, all of us recognize instantly when someone is nice to us or when we meet a nice person. Unfortunately, a common belief in our society is that people who are nice are inherently pleasant but weak. Not true. Most nice people are that way because they are strong and secure within themselves and know they can be human and effective.

Robert Levering, cofounder of the Great Place to Work Institute in San Francisco, along with his coauthors, Milton Moskowitz and Michael Katz, has written the books *The 100 Best Companies to Work for in America* and *A Great Place to Work,* which he describes as "where you trust the people you work for, have pride in what you do and enjoy the people you work with."

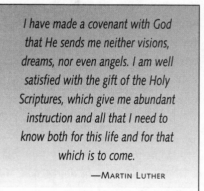

I have made a covenant with God that He sends me neither visions, dreams, nor even angels. I am well satisfied with the gift of the Holy Scriptures, which give me abundant instruction and all that I need to know both for this life and for that which is to come.

—MARTIN LUTHER

BARRA Investor Research study found that the one hundred best companies detailed in the book showed a 62 percent better annualized return in an index of comparable firms.

The U.S. Department of Labor compared seventy-five companies that use the traditional "command and control" philosophy with seventy-five "progressive organizations," that is, those with programs for worker involvement, training, teamwork, and profit sharing. Over five years the traditional firms showed an average annual increase in profits of 2.6 percent. The progressive firms showed a 10.8 percent increase. Sales growth was 10 percent versus 17.9 percent. Conclusion: Companies that are considerate of others and genuinely interested in their employees grow faster, sell more, and make more money.

I might add that these qualities of managing others are the same qualities that will enhance anyone's ride to the top.

What kind of people do managers like? Research indicates they like people who have a sense of humor; people who are dependable and have a ready smile; people who encourage others and have a positive attitude about life itself. They like people who take their work—but not themselves—seriously. Each of these qualities is a skill because it can be learned. Regardless of everything you've experienced, always remember that you can add to your career greatly by being a nice person with these qualities.

God helps me to live in a way that will please and honor Him so that I will always be doing good, kind things for others while learning to know God better and better. (Col. 1:10)

Wednesday's Child

SEVERAL YEARS AGO John Criswell, a local TV news anchor, hosted the program *Wednesday's Child*. Each Wednesday evening he presented one or more children who were available for adoption. Being a family man and father himself, John recognized the importance of giving children a stable home life to ensure that they have a legitimate chance of succeeding in life. Many of the children he presented were not "perfect children." Some had physical difficulties, some had mental disabilities, and some had both. John's objective was to have the children adopted by parents who should adopt them, not just parents who wanted a child. With that in mind, he always presented the children factually, lovingly expressing their liabilities and assets, and identifying the kinds of parents who would be best qualified to give the children the home, love, and care they needed.

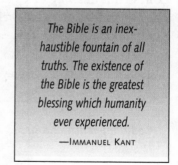

The Bible is an inexhaustible fountain of all truths. The existence of the Bible is the greatest blessing which humanity ever experienced.
—IMMANUEL KANT

Wednesday's Child was enormously successful, and an element of it came home to roost in 1997. John's wife, Elizabeth, was on a neighborhood journey when she spotted a disabled young man, probably in his early twenties, who was struggling to walk. She pulled over and offered him a ride. During the ride he revealed that he was interested in journalism. Elizabeth responded that her husband, John Criswell, was a television journalist. The young man broke out in a big grin and excitedly said, "Your husband literally changed my life! I am a Wednesday's Child."

Elizabeth Criswell got a warm glow as a result of the encounter. Her husband had given the young man a chance in life; she had given him a lift to his destination, and he had given her a substantial "lift" as well.

We have all thrown pebbles into a pond or lake and watched as the ever-widening circles spread onward and outward. In our daily lives we never know how a kind word, a sincere compliment, a lift to a disabled individual, etc. . . . will have an impact on someone we love down life's highway. George Matthew Adams expressed it this way: "He climbs highest who helps another up." The joy that Elizabeth Criswell felt because of something her husband, John, had done years earlier will bring a smile and perhaps even a teary eye to those who contemplate the kindness and compassion John Criswell displayed to Wednesday's Child.

God is my refuge and strength. He helps me when I am in trouble. *(Ps. 46:1)*

And the Winner Is . . .

THE 1998 WINTER OLYMPICS in Nagano, Japan, produced Tara Lipinski as the gold medal winner in figure skating. Michelle Kwan won the silver.

The event truly was one of the most exciting and closest competitions in the history of the Olympic Games. Eight of the nine judges placed the competitors within one-tenth of a point of each other; six of the judges rated Lipinski first in the long program. Had those six judges all graded Kwan a tenth of a point higher for technical merit, she would have won the gold medal handily. For that matter, Lipinski would have lost had any two of the judges given her a tenth of a point less for artistic impression.

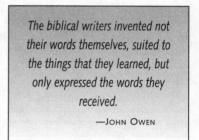

The biblical writers invented not their words themselves, suited to the things that they learned, but only expressed the words they received.

—JOHN OWEN

What made the minute difference that enabled Lipinski to win over Kwan? First, Lipinski opted to skate a tougher routine, which she performed nearly flawlessly. That always gives a competitor a slight advantage. Other reasons are more difficult to pinpoint. Both were completely committed; both had worked extremely hard; both have marvelous natural abilities, which they have developed to the utmost; both have outstanding attitudes. Did Lipinski work just a little harder, prepare herself a minute fraction better? No one can specifically answer those questions, but as often happens in life, the difference between the gold and the silver, between first and second, is often measured in minute increments. Both outstanding athletes have brilliant futures, and both will do extremely well financially. Not only have they done well in the Olympics, but with their continuing commitment, hard work, and character qualities, they will do well in life.

These two outstanding young women have taken seriously the old adage that yesterday is history, tomorrow is a mystery, and today is God's gift—that's why we call it the present. If each of us will realize that today really is a present, then we will use it to the fullest and accomplish many good things in our lives. As the psalmist beautifully put it, "This is the day which the LORD hath made; we will rejoice and be glad in it" (Ps. 118:24 KJV).

I am secure underneath the protecting shadow of God's wings and His strong right arm. (Ps. 63:7–8)

Here's a Role Model

CASEY MARTIN was a scholarship athlete at Stanford University and a teammate of Tiger Woods. He is one of the best ball strikers in golf, but he has a rare circulatory disorder that, according to his doctors, is getting progressively worse. Those who have seen him take the support stockings off his right leg are amazed that he can even walk. Within a matter of minutes his leg begins to swell, and soon it doubles in size. Constant pain is his twenty-four-hour-a-day companion.

Martin's doctors say his time as a golfer is probably limited because making a misstep, whether onto or off a golf cart, slipping on the steps leading to the tee or green, falling down a slope, even shopping in a grocery store, could end his career.

In addition, Casey Martin had to fight a serious court battle to force the Professional Golfers' Association (PGA) to permit him to ride a cart. This, despite the fact that many superb golfers believe that walking enhances their game, permitting them to get into a rhythm and flow of the game itself. Martin would love nothing better than to be able to

> The difference between reading and studying [the Bible] is like the difference between drifting in a boat and rowing toward a destination.
>
> —OSCAR FEUCHT

walk, but he could not survive the game if he were forced to. He's a courageous young man with a passion for golf and a real talent. He won the first Nike tournament he entered and was given permission to use a cart in that particular tournament.

Many of the big-time names on the PGA Tour believe it will destroy the "purity" of the game if he is permitted to ride. He has won a temporary victory and been granted the right to ride a cart. I hope the PGA lets it rest and this young man, who is such an outstanding example of the qualities our young people need, will be permitted to play the game he loves.

All of us have from time to time said that life is not fair, and that's true. To that, however, many will add the statement that God is good and all things work together for good to those who love God. Regardless of what Casey Martin does in his golf career, God can take his physical problems and use them in his life in a marvelous way. Paul told us in 2 Corinthians 12:7 (NLT), "I have received wonderful revelations from God. But to keep me from getting puffed up, I was given a thorn in my flesh, a messenger from Satan to torment me and keep me from getting proud."

I am an ordinary, weak human being, but I don't use human plans and methods to win my battles. I use God's mighty weapons, not those made by man, to knock down the devil's stronghold. (2 Cor. 10:3–4)

Communicating with Your Mate

IT'S A WELL-ESTABLISHED fact that men and women are different. Nevertheless, we still treat each other as if we're the same.

To get along better with your mate, you need to understand the difference and communicate differently. For example: Wife, odds are good that on many occasions you've asked your husband to do something, and he readily agreed to follow through. The basic problem is that although his intentions were good, he got involved in other things, and his good intentions went down the drain. Frequent reminders or, to put it a little uglier, nagging, may enter the picture. That seldom makes for a happy marriage.

Solution: Give your husband a note saying, "Honey, would you please stop by the dry cleaners, which is across the street from the grocery store, on the way home this evening and pick up my cleaning? I also need two cans

> The ordinary Christian, with a Bible in his hand, can say that the majority is wrong.
> —FRANCIS SCHAEFFER

of tomatoes so we can have vegetable soup for dinner." He will appreciate it, and odds will go up dramatically that he'll follow through. Men respond more to the written word than they do to the spoken word.

Husband, if you want to ring your wife's bell, turn her on, and draw closer to her, verbalize your request and express your appreciation and love at the same time. Say something like, "Honey, I'd really love it if you would stop by and pick up my dry cleaning across the street from the grocery store when you pick up the two cans of tomatoes we need for the vegetable soup."

The same message—one written, one verbalized. Use this idea, and chances are good that you'll eliminate a lot of miscommunication and squabbles and have a happier marriage.

Communicating with your mate is extremely important. You communicate by your spoken word, the look in your eyes, the touch of your hand, the consideration you show in putting your mate first. God gives us marvelous communication advice: "Be kind to each other, tenderhearted, forgiving one another, just as God through Christ has forgiven you" (Eph. 4:32 NLT). Since the Bible clearly states that Jesus Christ is the same yesterday, today, and forever, we can rest assured that His Word is not going to change. He communicated the greatest love message ever delivered: "For God so loved the world, that he gave his only begotten Son, that whosoever believeth in him should not perish, but have everlasting life" (John 3:16 KJV). What a marvelous gift to all of us!

The wife of my youth is a blessing, and I rejoice her. Her charms and tender embraces satisfy me, and her love alone fills me with delight. (Prov. 5:18–19)

Week Eleven

The Immigrant's Attitude

THE JUNE 17, 1997, issue of the *Los Angeles Times* told about a study conducted by Michigan State and Princeton Universities. The study portrays children of immigrants as quick to learn English, which is contrary to concerns raised by antiimmigration groups. The study followed five thousand children in San Diego and Miami starting in 1991. The sample represented the immigrant population in terms of national origin, and the children had at least one foreign-born parent.

> To me the greatest thing that has happened on this earth of ours is the rise of the human race to the vision of God. That story of the human rise to what I call the vision of God is the story which is told in the Bible.
> —JAN CHRISTIAAN SMUTS

Grade point averages were slightly higher than the district's 133,000 students as a whole. For example, in the twelfth grade, 46 percent of all students had at least a B average, while 50 percent of immigrant children performed that well. Perhaps the most startling difference, however, was that fewer than 6 percent of the immigrants' children dropped out, compared with 16 percent districtwide. "Some immigrant groups and their children are doing well and seem poised to join the middle-class mainstream—if they are not there already," said Michigan State sociologist Ruben G. Rumbaut, a project coordinator.

Rumbaut also found that about two-thirds of the students read English "very well," based on self-reports and test scores, and only about a quarter read another language more fluently. The study indicated that American culture might erode the work ethic of immigrants' children. The longer they lived in the United States, the less time they spent on homework.

That last sentence says a lot about our work ethic and the fact that our associates influence us in many ways. Maybe if there were more immigrants, they would improve our work and study habits, which would benefit everyone.

I do my very best in whatever I do so I have the personal satisfaction of work well done. Then I don't need to compare myself with anyone else. (Gal. 6:4)

Eating for Success

LARRY BLEIBERG, a writer about education and the Dallas Independent School District for the *Dallas Morning News,* reported on a survey showing that teenagers who regularly share meals with their families are three times more likely to say their home life is happy and close most of the time than teens who do not have meals with their families. He also noted that the frequent family diners are more satisfied with their prospects for the future than classmates who rarely eat with their families. They are twice as likely to devote long hours to homework and much less likely to have premarital sex or consider suicide.

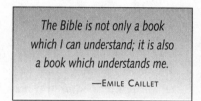

The Bible is not only a book which I can understand; it is also a book which understands me.

—EMILE CAILLET

Who's Who Among American High School Students conducted the survey of high school students. "When a family has dinner together they're doing a lot more than eating," said Paul Krouse, founder and publisher of the publication that honors high-achieving teens. "They're really sharing their lives. They're demonstrating an interest in each other." The survey, taken in the spring of 1995, was based on responses from 3,351 teenagers who had an A or B average and were considered high achievers. Other surveys have had similar results.

Actually, it's not that involved. Two, three, or four times a week of eating together can make a difference, whether it's Sunday brunch, Saturday lunch, or Friday night dinner. This difference-making routine truly offers a wide range of benefits.

Bleiberg pointed out that at mealtime parents can find out about their children's problems or worries. Likewise, children get a better understanding of their parents when everyone shares his daily life. Krouse concluded with an encouraging word for single parents: "We don't have any statistics that tell us that a single-parent family is going to perform worse. A single mom or a single dad can accomplish an awful lot."

I watch my tongue, do not lie, turn from all known sin, spend my time in doing good, and work hard at living in peace [my responsibility] because I want a long, good life [God's promise]. (Ps. 34:12–14)

Virginity Is "In"

ALTHOUGH TEENS are credited with saying, "Everybody's doing it," and the media seem to promote that image, many teenagers are recognizing that virginity, as one girl put it, "is wickedly cool."

On a *PrimeTime Live* special, Diane Sawyer interviewed a number of teens who were sexually active. At the conclusion of the program Sawyer pointed out that all of those kids later told her they wished they had waited for marriage to get involved in sex.

An article by Irene Sege in the *Boston Globe* reported that high school health teacher Donna Georges heard something she wasn't seeing a few years ago: "There are girls now who are saying out loud—and that's the difference, saying out loud—that 'I'm not ready for this.'"

> Disregard the study of God and you sentence yourself to stumble and blunder through life, blindfolded, as it were, with no sense of direction and no understanding of what surrounds you.
>
> —J. I. PACKER

Several religious organizations, including the Southern Baptist Convention, support the campaign True Love Waits, and teens by the tens of thousands are pledging to wait until they are married for sexual intimacy. Those who have already been involved in sexual activity are pledging to discontinue it until they find the mate of their choice.

Today more and more people are being invited into public schools to counsel and encourage the boys and girls to wait, pointing out the obvious benefits that go with abstaining from sex until they are mature enough to handle the relationship and have chosen a lifetime mate with whom to share their most priceless gift. I encourage every parent, newspaper, and school to publicize the trend and encourage young men and women to follow this route. It's a much safer, surer way to major accomplishments in life.

I keep a close watch on all I do and think and stay true to what is right [my responsibility], and God is blessing me and using me to help others [God's promise]. (1 Tim. 4:16)

Movement or Gravity?

MOTIVATION IS basically movement. Negative thinking is gravity. One moves you up, and the other holds you down. Unfortunately, negative thinking takes less effort than positive thinking. However, consider this: when we shot that rocket into space, it took more fuel to get it through the first fifty thousand feet than it did to make the rest of the trip to the moon. Once you get airborne, start to move upward, and get out of the negative crowd below, the rest of the journey is much easier. It takes focus and effort to break away from those who are content with where they are, but once you do, you are able to increase your speed, even as you get older. That's exciting.

> After reading the doctrines of Plato, Socrates, or Aristotle, we feel that the specific difference between their words and Christ's is the difference between an inquiry and a revelation.
>
> —JOSEPH PARKER

How do you get motivated? Reach into your pocket or desk, pull out a pen and a piece of paper, and write down at least ten things for which you are grateful: your health, clothing, home, automobile, family, friends—whatever. Next, make a list of the things you would like to have: new car, better job, happier marriage, or a new suit. Now ask yourself, What can

I do to acquire these things? Maybe you need to read an inspirational book, get more education, or develop new contacts. Remember that motivation is basically movement, and the statement that "logic will not change an emotion but action will" is a valid one.

We've all had the experience of not wanting to do something we had to do, but in the process of doing it we discovered it wasn't that bad, and actually, it was fun. All of that started with a first step. Speaker Joe Sabah wisely observed, "You don't have to be great to start, but you have to start to be great." The first step makes the second one easier, and before you realize it, you are on a roll.

I sing to the Lord because He has blessed me so richly. (Ps. 13:6)

Dads Are Important

TAMARA HENRY'S ARTICLE in the October 3, 1997, issue of *USA Today* is exciting and very revealing. She reported on a study by the Education Department indicating that children are more likely to get A's and less likely to repeat a grade or be expelled if fathers are highly involved in their schools. This is true whether the fathers live with their children or whether the mothers are also active. Incidentally, involvement is defined as participation in school meetings, teacher conferences, a class meeting, or volunteering.

I suspect a major reason for the child's higher academic standing is that the father communicates to the child, "You're important to me, so your education is important." Research also shows that when the teachers see that the father is involved and genuinely concerned about his child's education, they do a better job with the student.

This study was based on interviews with parents and guardians

> I have heard a few Greek scholars say that when they first read Plato, they found it a mirror for their souls. That may be. But they never found in Plato salvation from their sins, nor a sinless Redeemer, nor the absolute assurance of eternal life and of resurrection after death. Only the Bible offers you that.
>
> —WILBUR SMITH

111

of nearly seventeen thousand students. In two-parent households where both parents were highly involved, 51 percent of the children got mostly A's; however, 48 percent did so when only the father was highly involved. Forty-four percent did when just the mother was highly involved. Only 27 percent got mostly A's if neither parent was very involved. When involvement by both parents was low, a child's chance of success was dramatically reduced. For this particular study, the margin of error was less than 1 percent.

When our kids see that we really care, they learn to care as well, and they get an education, which is increasingly important. So, parents, get involved, and someday your kids just might raise kids who will make you proud grandparents.

God has filled me with His mighty, glorious strength, so I can keep going, always full of the joy of the Lord, no matter what happens. (Col. 1:11)

Week Twelve

Now What Do You Say?

THE COUPLE were driving through a lonely stretch of back-country and decided to stop at a cabin for a drink of water and to make conversation with the grizzled old settler. The husband visited with the man on the porch, noting, "Seems pretty lonesome around here."

The older man shifted the chew in his toothless face, spat onto the yard below, and said, "Solitude is a state of mind which effectuates its reactionary tendencies and inoculates those with hypersensitivity. However, having been a victim of claustrophobia during my adolescence, I find habitation in the environment of nature's wonders not only serene and desirous, but fundamentally mandatory."

> Just as all things upon earth represent and image forth all the realities of another world, so the Bible is one mighty representative of the whole spiritual life of humanity.
>
> —HELEN KELLER

The couple left in silence, and after a short drive down the road the wife turned and asked her husband, "Well, why don't you say something, Einstein?"

Chances are pretty good that this incident is merely the figment of a creative imagination to give all of us cause to smile, ponder, and perhaps laugh a little. Sometimes, however, we are somewhat taken aback when someone speaks to be politically correct and ends up saying nothing of substance, or when someone who is impressed with the extent of his own vocabulary wants to dazzle and impress us with his words, hoping to make us think he is really bright. But the only person impressed is the one who is doing the talking! Good communicators express themselves so clearly that there is no room for confusion in the minds of the listeners. When you express yourself clearly, you benefit both speaker and listener, and that gives both parties a better chance to attain and maintain an up, up attitude.

I love the Lord my God with all of my heart and with all my soul and with all my strength. (Deut. 6:5)

Taking Off the Makeup

IT SEEMS that research is done on just about everything nowadays. Some of it is exciting, beneficial, and fascinating. For example, research now indicates that women who ritualistically take off their makeup before going to bed are less inclined to insomnia than those who forgo this routine.

It's not the removal of the makeup that allows the women to sleep better, but the routine that allows them to taper off from the hectic pace of the day. In most cases, the makeup is removed quietly and unhurriedly. The very slowing down enables the person to get into bed in a more relaxed frame of mind, which helps her to drift off to sleep more quickly.

> A man may read the figures on the dial, but he cannot tell how the day goes unless the sun is shining on it; so we may read the Bible over, but we cannot learn to purpose till the spirit of God shines upon it and into our hearts.
>
> —THOMAS WATSON

This message is not about taking off makeup, but about the routine involved. Most men don't have makeup to take off. However, developing their own procedure or routine to slow down their pace at the end of the day will help them to sleep better as well. My favorite preparation for bed is to spend a few minutes listening to music.

Soothing melodies are particularly good for me, and my favorites are some of the great gospel songs. I find them most comforting. They slow me down, force me to think, fill my gratitude bucket, and overall give me a much better chance of not letting the daily grind keep me from going up, up, up in a down, down world.

I can do everything God asks me to do with the help of Christ who gives me strength and power. (Phil. 4:13)

Compassion Is Good Business

WRITING IN the *Dallas Morning News*, April 13, 1998, Michael Vandergriff recognized Roger Enrico, the chief executive at PepsiCo, for donating his yearly salary to a scholarship fund for the children of his employees who were making less than $60,000 a year. I'm confident some cynics will say, "Well, he's rich and has all those stock options." That's true, but those stock options are valuable only if the stock goes up.

Many years ago Mary Kay Ash made the observation that everyone walks around with an invisible sign around his neck saying, "Make me feel important." Can you just imagine how the PepsiCo employees feel, knowing that the man in charge of their company

> Sink the Bible to the bottom of the ocean, and still man's obligations to God would be unchanged.—He would have the same path to tread, only his lamp and his guide would be gone;—the same voyage to make, but his chart and compass would be overboard.
>
> —HENRY WARD BEECHER

wants to help them and their children enjoy a better life? I agree with Vandergriff when he says that PepsiCo employees will be motivated to give their best effort and their best effort will increase productivity. Increased productivity and commitment from the employees will reduce turnover, one of the biggest expenses any company or organization encounters. A productivity increase will improve profitability, and profitability will mean that Enrico is going to do quite well. However, I believe he wanted to do it because he could do it and felt that it was the right thing to do.

It is my conviction that Enrico's action caused more of a buzz and a greater positive attitude among the people than anything that had happened at that company or any other company in a long time. And that will give a lot of people in the organization an up, up, up attitude because it gives them hope—and hope sees the invisible, feels the intangible, and achieves the impossible.

God reaches down from heaven and rescues me. He delivers me from deep waters and from the power of my enemies. (Ps. 144:7)

Bruce and the Banana

A TRULY outstanding and different golfer on the PGA Tour is Dallasite Bruce Lietzke. He picks the few tournaments he wishes to play and is a big money winner. He never practices, and sometimes he doesn't pick up a golf club for months. He says his swing is part of himself, and since he has it right where he wants it, he doesn't need to practice.

> To my early knowledge of the Bible I owe the best part of my taste in literature, and the most precious, and on the whole, the one essential part of my education.
>
> —JOHN RUSKIN

His caddy decided to test him, so at the end of one season, he slipped a banana in Lietzke's golf bag. Three months later when he opened the bag again, there was the dried-up banana.

Lietzke takes this approach because he has his priorities in order. He plays ten events a year to keep his hand in the game until he qualifies for the Senior PGA Tour in 2001. Until then, he says, the most important things in life for him are his wife, Rosemarie; son, Stephen; and daughter, Christine. In 1997 Lietzke didn't play a single event from June to October so that he could stay at home and caddie for his son, who was a junior golfer, and coach his daughter in softball.

When Lietzke started his career, he played only 225 events from 1976 to 1988. He said that when he got married, his interest was in his family. Despite his limited schedule, he has thirteen career wins. He started 1998 in the Bob Hope Classic and finished the tourney tied for first and then lost in a play-off to Fred Couples. When Lietzke hits the Senior Tour, I believe he's going to be a big winner. In the meantime he is enjoying life with his family.

The Lord has plans for me and they are good. They give me hope and a future. (Jer. 29:11)

Looking Through Love's Eyes

GOETHE MADE a rather profound statement when he said, "If I treat you as you are, you will remain as you are. If I treat you as if you were what you could be, that is what you will become." Those words of long ago express in a unique way what love is about. As I reread them for the umpteenth time, I think of the love in a family and the way we see each other. Looking at your mate as alive, well, and alert rather than nosy, or seeing him or her as exercising good judgment and thrift instead of being shallow and stingy, will have a profound impact on your relationship. If you think of your mate as being expressive instead of talkative, and if you consider him or her sensitive and caring rather than touchy, your respect and admiration for your mate will grow, and you will develop a deeper love, appreciation, and understanding of him or her.

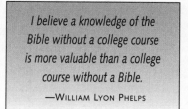

I believe a knowledge of the Bible without a college course is more valuable than a college course without a Bible.
—WILLIAM LYON PHELPS

When you take that approach, you will have mastered one of the great lessons of life—namely, that when you love someone, you do not react to the symptoms of behavior, but you respond to the need that your mate might have. In this process you will learn that love will always give you the benefit of the doubt. Over a period of time you will realize that you do that not because you want to do what is right, but because you have become that kind of person.

The underlying message behind all of this is that you can change, and in the process you will have a substantial influence on the life of the other person. Each of you will win, and as a couple, you will win. That's the way to beat the daily grind.

I will praise the Lord and constantly speak of His grace and glory, and will boast of His kindness to me, no matter what happens. (Ps. 34:1–2)

Week Thirteen

Self-Talk for Employment

ROGER MAURICE of Mechanicsburg, Ohio, had a problem. In November of 1994 his job was eliminated as a result of staff reductions, and he had to find another position. He admitted that for a brief period of time he had a bad case of stinkin' thinkin'. Six weeks later he received two phone calls scheduling job interviews. One of the jobs was something he knew very little about, and the other was a job almost identical to the one he had held for nearly ten years.

He knew his chances of getting the first job were slim because of his lack of experience. But Roger really wanted the other job, so he decided to use the first interview as a warm-up for the second one. First, he learned the qualities necessary for success in either job, wrote them on an index card, and started claiming them for himself several times a day. In preparation he also

> I have always believed in the inspiration of the Holy Scriptures, whereby they have become the expression to man of the Word and Will of God.
>
> —WARREN G. HARDING

reviewed Les Giblin's book, *Skill with People*, especially the chapter "How to Skillfully Make a Good First Impression." This information and the self-talk gave him considerable confidence.

The first interview went well, but the second one was the clincher. As the interview ended, the interviewer asked him if he had anything else to say. Roger took a deep breath and said, "If you select me, I will do a good job for you," and he left the interview knowing he had done well.

The next week he received the coveted phone call telling him the job was his. He says preparation made the difference. Today, Roger Maurice has lots to smile about, and if you prepare as Roger did, you will too.

There is no sex sin, greed, or impurity in me. Dirty stories, foul talk, and coarse jokes are not for me. I think of God's goodness and am thankful. (Eph. 5:3–4)

Chance Has No Memory

IN JANUARY OF 1998, Lleyton Hewitt, an Australian high school tennis player, became the lowest-ranked player (550) ever to win an ATP (Association of Tennis Professionals) Tour event.

What are the odds that number 550 would beat players who were ranked in the top 50 in the world and many of them in the top 20? I wonder if Hewitt honestly thought he had a chance, or was he playing for the thrill of competing against some of the best? Did he figure he had nothing to lose? I find it difficult to believe he entered the tournament with any degree of confidence that he was going to win.

He won. I'm certain after he won the first match he felt good, and when he won the second one, I believe his confidence grew dramatically.

Hewitt obviously took a chance, entered the event, and came out the winner. One difference between those who do great things and those who do only average or mediocre things

> I cannot too greatly emphasize the importance and value of Bible study—more important than ever before in these days of uncertainties, when men and women are apt to decide questions from the standpoint of expediency rather than on the eternal principles laid down by God, Himself.
>
> —JOHN WANAMAKER

is that big winners are willing to take a chance—but they're not gamblers. The farmer is a risk taker when he plants his crop. He is at the complete mercy of the weather and the marketplace, and yet it would certainly be a gamble not to plant the crop at all. That would make him a sure loser. He takes the risks, and the benefits, over the long haul, come his way.

When you're confronted with the choice of taking a risk or not, ask yourself, What do I have to gain by winning, and what do I have to lose if I lose? If you can handle the worst that could happen, I encourage you to take the calculated risk. Chances are good, you'll develop an upbeat attitude that will help you throughout life.

The Lord does amazing things for me. He is a source of wonder and joy, and refreshes me. (Ps. 126:2–3)

Fascinating—But Wrong

MOST OF US grew up believing that Charles Lindbergh was the first man to fly nonstop across the Atlantic. We've read the books; we've seen the movie; and although he truly was a real-life American hero, he was not the first man to fly the Atlantic.

In 1919, eight years before Lindbergh crossed the Atlantic, Capt. John Alcock and Lt. Arthur Whitten-Broun flew from Newfoundland to Galway, Ireland.

Another fascinating non-fact is that the heart works all the time. If you are seventy years old, for roughly forty years of your life your heart has been completely at rest. And consider this: many times you hear someone described as a workaholic who works all the time. But no one works 168 hours each week. Many of the "truths" we've believed for years simply are not true. Perhaps we're not as far off as "the world is flat" concept that

> *I believe that the Bible is to be understood and received in the plain and obvious meaning of its passages; for I cannot persuade myself that a book intended for the instruction and conversion of the whole world should cover its true meaning in any such mystery and doubt that none but critics and philosophers can discover it.*
>
> —DANIEL WEBSTER

was around for a few thousand years. Nevertheless, many untruths remain.

You may be wondering what difference it makes. Well, it really doesn't make a lot of difference, but it could possibly alert some of us to the fact that we need to be careful about being dogmatic in many of our statements because sometimes what we've been taught as fact all of our lives isn't factual. One way to have a more pleasant, productive, and enjoyable life is to get the facts, and when you hear something contrary to what you've always believed, you should listen with a receptive mind. Not only will you win more friends with that approach, but you also could well end up with more facts that are true.

I try to be good, loving, and kind, so I find life, godliness, and honor. (Prov. 21:21)

The Most Desirable Employees

DR. TONY ZEISS, president of Central Piedmont Community College in Charlotte, North Carolina, has identified through research the characteristics of the most desirable employees or job candidates. A positive attitude is the most important characteristic. The most often promoted employees have high job performance, exhibit good corporate citizenship behavior, and are committed to the organization.

Additional research reveals that promotions occurred when the employees viewed the organization's problems as their own. The abilities to foster positive working relationships and to lead others contribute to career success.

Happy people are promoted more often than neutral or negative people; they are also healthier. Workers under age thirty are happier and more satisfied with their jobs than any other age-group. Baby boomers are the most negative. One hundred percent of six hundred top executives in a 1994 study by

> Voltaire spoke of the Bible as a short-lived book. He said that within a hundred years it would pass from common use. Not many people read Voltaire today, but his house has been packed with Bibles as a depot of a Bible society.
>
> —BRUCE BARTON

Hodge Crouin and Associates believe that humor has a positive impact in their business, and 95 percent said, all things being equal, they would hire candidates with a sense of humor.

There is a direct relationship between employee attitude, customer satisfaction, and employee turnover, and the shared attitudes of employees affect morale and productivity.

These results are not too surprising, and yet sometimes we overlook the obvious: a positive attitude has a positive effect on your life.

I know that nothing is perfect except Your words, and I love and think about them all day long. They make me wiser than my enemies because I use them as my constant guide. (Ps. 119:96–98)

Women Are Dependable

ACCORDING TO the *Wall Street Journal*, between 1989 and 1995 more than fifteen million new businesses were started in America, more than half of them by women who had several things in common.

First, in virtually every case they had a great financial need. Second, these women had no specific skills for starting a business. Third, nearly all of them started what is called a trust business, which means they had to say to their customers, "Give me the money, and I will deliver the goods or services at a later date." I find it exciting that there have been few, if any, prosecutions of these women for not delivering the goods.

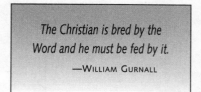

The Christian is bred by the Word and he must be fed by it.
—WILLIAM GURNALL

Apparently many of them needed income because of divorce or desertion or downsizing, which put them on the unemployment rolls. Instead of moaning and groaning, whining and complaining, or going on welfare, they recognized an opportunity to begin something on their own that they would never have had the courage to do had necessity not entered the picture. As the old saying goes, many of these women had been handed lemons, but they chose to make lemonade.

The rest of the story is that in the process of creating these new businesses, most of which were initially one-person operations, many of them expanded and provided employment opportunities for others. I believe this is one reason our economy is so good today, and unemployment is at its lowest level in several decades. These women had something to frown about when necessity forced them into the marketplace, but today because of the way they've handled it, they have much to be grateful for.

I stand firm and keep a strong grip on God's truth and have everlasting comfort and hope, which I don't deserve. God helps me in every good thing I say and do. (2 Thess. 2:15–17)

Week Fourteen

It Don't Matter

YEARS AGO I heard a speaker, whose name I have forgotten, work the refrain "it don't matter" throughout his entire talk. He did it humorously and effectively. It was a version of "don't sweat the small stuff," and it made sense because who will remember those petty difficulties a year or two down the road?

A wise person commented, "There is no limit to what we can do if we don't worry about who gets the credit." Unfortunately, many people still labor under the illusion that they've got to do everything because they can't depend on anyone else to do it right. In his beautiful book *The Great Lover's Manifesto*, Dave Grant pointed out that the atti-

> *The Bible is one of the greatest blessings bestowed by God on the children of men.—It has God for its author; salvation for its end, and truth without any mixture for its matter.—It is all pure, all sincere; nothing too much; nothing wanting.*
>
> —LOCKE

tude, "If I don't do it, it won't be done right," is a jealous, fear-filled attitude that keeps people stunted. The real issue may be, "If I don't do it, it won't be done *my way*."

That's certainly a sobering thought and one that should give all of us pause to wonder, particularly the perfectionists who believe there are two ways to do anything: their way or the wrong way. These people, across the board, are generally frustrated and seldom end up developing and using their full potential. Perfection is hard to achieve. However, good effort and a sincere conviction that you've done your best are hallmarks of the big winners in life. I love the expression, "Success is honest effort, fully expended, in quest of a worthy ideal." When you take that approach, the results will be so significant, you won't need to worry about who gets the credit or whether the effort was perfect.

I have thoroughly tested God's promises and found them pure; therefore, I love His Word. (Ps. 119:140)

The If-Only's of Life

THE MASTERS GOLF TOURNAMENT is truly one of the most prestigious events on the sports calendar. Many golfers say it is *the* most important single event. Mark O'Meara won the 1998 Masters, now wears the green jacket of the champion, and has a lot of "green" to show for his victory.

Mark O'Meara is a deserving champion, but let's look at some of the if-only's of the four days. O'Meara won by sinking a twenty-foot putt on the eighteenth green. That was the first time he had taken the lead in the tournament. Had he missed that putt, it would have forced a play-off with David Duval and Fred Couples. There also would have been a vic-

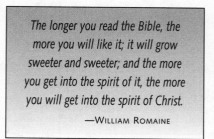

The longer you read the Bible, the more you will like it; it will grow sweeter and sweeter; and the more you get into the spirit of it, the more you will get into the spirit of Christ.

—WILLIAM ROMAINE

tory for Fred Couples if only he had not hit that ball in Rae's Creek and ended up taking a double bogey. David Duval would have won the tournament—or at least been in the play-off—if only he had not three-putted one of the finishing holes from just twenty feet away. Tiger Woods would have won if only he had putted in the 1998 Masters as he did in the 1997 Masters.

Life is filled with if-only's. "If only" we'd called earlier, the relationship could have been salvaged. "If only" we'd started our savings plan earlier, we could have already retired. "If only" we'd set a better example for our children, perhaps they would not have gotten involved in drugs, promiscuous sex, or crime.

We can't look back and change one iota of our history. But if we let our past teach us and not beat us, we won't have to look back and say "if only" too many times.

I love the Lord because He hears my prayers and answers them. He bends down and listens so I will pray as long as I live. (Ps. 116:1–2)

Turn It Off

A FASCINATING ARTICLE in *Parade Magazine* of April 12, 1998, provided exciting data about the advantages of turning off the television set for one week and tying a ribbon in front of it to remind the family that it's off-limits. Many of the kids didn't think it was a good idea, even saying, "You've got to be nuts!" but later reported that they got through the week, and they did well.

After that week of total abstinence from television, most people recognized the incredible benefits: more time to talk, read, exercise, be together, and do more

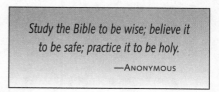

Study the Bible to be wise; believe it to be safe; practice it to be holy.
—ANONYMOUS

creative thinking. It's not what TV does to you, but what it prevents you from doing that is the most destructive thing about it.

National TV-Turnoff Week was started in 1995 by Henry Labalme, cofounder of TV-Free America, a nonprofit group that organizes the event. Today, organizations such as the American Medical Association and Children's Defense Fund also participate. One objective, to improve literacy, is supported by the Literacy Volunteers of America. National TV-Turnoff Week is now observed in fifty thousand schools throughout the country.

At Public School 51 in the Bronx, New York, Principal Esther

Forrest believes that overexposure to TV can harm her students' ability to learn. She explained, "Things move so fast on TV, I think it shortens kids' attention spans."

Lisa Hendrickson, a freshman at the University of Wisconsin, observed, "Anyone who did well in school and athletics or other activities practically never watched TV." Labalme does not deny that TV programming has some merit, but he believes that "people who turn off their TVs begin to discover how marvelous the real world is."

I use Your words as a flashlight to light the path ahead of me to keep me from stumbling. (Ps. 119:105)

Causing Good Things to Happen

SHANTHONY LEWIS from Detroit, Texas, reaped the rewards of commitment, responsibility, hard work, and just plain being a super, nice young woman. The shy seventeen-year-old was academically gifted and athletically talented. However, she was struggling to live on a welfare check and make a home for her younger sister because their mother was in jail.

Her story hit the *Dallas Morning News*, and within two weeks four colleges had offered full or partial scholarships to Shanthony, who was ranked third in her East Texas class. An anonymous donor pledged to pay for four years of education at the college of her choice, others sent checks for substantial amounts of money, and yet another $2,500 was earmarked for

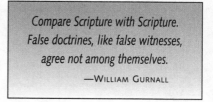

Compare Scripture with Scripture. False doctrines, like false witnesses, agree not among themselves.

—WILLIAM GURNALL

her college expenses. The gifts included personal items like a new pair of size thirteen sandals, which was a significant gift for a six-three teenager with hard-to-fit feet. She received a fancy evening bag to match her black satin prom dress. One family sent a big Easter basket with goodies for her six-year-old sister, Kyatta. Someone sent twenty pairs of designer socks; someone else took Shanthony shopping for her college wardrobe. Many nice, compassionate, generous people exemplified what is good in life. The shy teenager was overwhelmed with the attention she received and the generosity of so many people.

What a refreshing story from a small town and a talented young lady committed to excellence and doing what is right. Not only did she have lots to be up, up, up about, but just hearing about it gives all of us a great example to follow and helps us to have daily hope.

I will sing to the Lord as long as I live and will praise God to my last breath, for He is the source of all my joy. (Ps. 104:33)

Go Lights, Warms, and Strong Ends

IN THIS GREAT LAND of ours, too many people are using negative expressions such as "stoplights." In reality the electrical appliances on street corners are put there to make traffic go more safely, smoothly, and rapidly. We spend something like twenty-seven hours each year in front of those lights, waiting for the right color so we can move forward.

My friend and brother, Bernie Lofchick from Winnipeg, Canada, is the most positive man I've ever met. He's so positive, he's never had a cold. He says that's negative. He calls them "warms." He doesn't talk about the weekend; he calls it the "strong end." He makes no reference to stoplights; he calls them "go lights."

Your question might well be, "Is that really necessary?" The answer is no, you can be mediocre without it. Your response could be, "What do you mean, mediocre? I'm the president of my own company!" or "I'm worth seven million dollars!" or "I have my Ph.D." or "I was number one in sales." Well, bully for you! I still say mediocre because success is not measured by

> It is a belief in the Bible, the fruit of deep meditation, which has served me as the guide of my moral and literary life. I have found it a capital safely invested, and richly productive of interest.
>
> —GOETHE

what you do compared to what others can do. Success is measured by what you do compared to what you are capable of doing.

I'm not saying you must be the best in the world because there can be only one who is the best. But I'm talking about being number one with the most important person in your future, and that is you. That way, when you look into the mirror every night and say, "Today I gave it my best shot," you will find that what you do is more than good enough to accomplish some incredible objectives in your life.

When doubts fill my mind and my heart is in turmoil, God quiets me and gives me renewed hope and cheer . . . He is my fortress, the mighty rock where I can hide. (Ps. 94:19, 22)

Week Fifteen

Backing Up to Go Forward

IN THIS HIGH-TECH AGE of ours, when so many things are done via computer, the Internet, and fax, one of the major players in the accelerated game has reversed field and made significant progress.

Digital Equipment Corporation has replaced computers with human beings to answer the phones. The company made the switch for the same reason it installed the computer phone-answering system in the first place—to improve efficiency. Results have been spectacular. Customer satisfaction, as measured

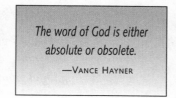

The word of God is either absolute or obsolete.
—VANCE HAYNER

by being able to reach the right person, shot up from 73 percent to 97 percent, and misdirected calls have fallen to just 1 percent. Additionally, the caller who is misdirected receives a personal apology from the one who misdirected him in the first place. What a novel idea!

Many of us don't think it's novel at all. We point out, with a degree of smug satisfaction, that that's the only way we've ever done it because our parents and grandparents taught that procedure.

It reminds me of the corny old joke that made the rounds when big dairies first used electric milkers and milk production went down because the cows preferred the personal touch. I believe there was a grain of truth in that humor, but I can speak with confidence when I say that people definitely prefer the human touch. That's one reason why at our company you will always hear a person answer the phone unless the lines are completely jammed—and then it's only a matter of a few seconds before live service is available. When the office is not open, we believe it is efficient to use our automated answering system to serve our customers better. Our clients tell us that gives them lots to smile about, so take the personal touch approach and your clients will say nice things about you and to you.

God alone is my refuge, my place of safety, and I trust Him. He protects me from every trap and fatal plague. He shields me with His wings, and His faithful promises are my armor. (Ps. 91:2–4)

Maybe You Should Travel

POSSIBLY AS YOU looked at the title, your first thought was, *How can I do that? It takes time, it costs money, I'm too busy,* and so on. Realistically speaking, I'm convinced you can go to those far-away places with those strange-sounding names.

Many of us have already had the privilege of physically going to a lot of those faraway places, but millions more—including you—also take those trips. In addition to my physical travels, I've had the privilege of traveling back in time as I've read of the things that happened hundreds and even thousands of years ago. I've also had the privilege of reading many of the forecasts of what will be happening in the future. On a daily basis I see change taking place. I read about projections and observe that things are radically different today from what they were even five or ten years ago. My travels in my mind and imagination enable me to imagine what it would be like to walk on the moon, as our astronauts have done, or explore the depths of the oceans, as some have been privileged to do.

> In what light soever we regard the Bible, whether with reference to revelation, to history, or to morality, it is an invaluable and inexhaustible mine of knowledge and virtue.
>
> —JOHN QUINCY ADAMS

We can create via the spoken and written word many bits of useful, inspirational, and informational ideas that, when properly used, will enable us to physically take those trips that for the moment are only dreams. Obviously that requires action, and one of the most important actions is to become well informed through the thousands of books and maps available in our public libraries, through bookstores, as well as the Internet. Take advantage of our educational resources, and chances are good that someday you can physically take those trips you have dreamed about. Thinking about it and developing a plan to do something about it will encourage you and give you renewed hope.

———————————

I rejoice because I put my trust in You, and I shout for joy because You defend me. I am filled with happiness because You bless me and protect me with Your shield of love. (Ps. 5:11–12)

Exciting Things Are Happening

VIRTUALLY EVERYONE has heard something about Promise Keepers, an organization committed to teaching men how to be better and more responsible husbands and fathers. Interest has been tremendous; results have been dramatic.

Something similar and just as exciting was made available to women. In Nashville 19,600 women attended the first "Renewing the Heart" Conference. Twenty thousand women who had requested tickets could not attend because it was sold out. "Renewing the Heart" conferences also took place in Greensboro, San Antonio, Philadelphia, and Tampa. The cost was minimal, allowing almost any woman to attend.

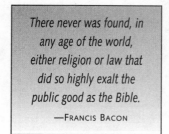

There never was found, in any age of the world, either religion or law that did so highly exalt the public good as the Bible.
—FRANCIS BACON

What was it all about? It was about giving women hope and encouragement through spiritual renewal and fellowship. Dr. James Dobson, founder of Focus on the Family and sponsor of "Renewing the Heart," described it as a place of respite, a chance to be still: "For women who are weary, pulled in a hundred different directions by the competing interests of family, work, church, finances and personal growth needs, this conference is a refuge, a time of restoration, and a chance to re-evaluate God's priorities for life. For those who are already well-equipped and well-nourished for the journey, it is a chance to be encouraged and encourage others." It was values oriented and family centered, with a strong emphasis on the importance of faith.

The headlines shout for a return to our country's foundational values. I'm excited about organizations that are committed to strengthening the family and providing means with which to cope with the pressures of modern family life.

I reverence God, so I have deep strength and my children have a place of refuge and security and I have a fountain of life. (Prov. 14:26–27)

A Formula for Success

OVER THE YEARS I've come to realize that some specifics help you enjoy success in each area of your life. You start with the right mental attitude, and I speak of more than positive thinking. Attitude is not everything, but it is the beginning point for success. With the right mental attitude you will recognize that you need to learn specific skills. A positive-thinking doctor, without the necessary education, would not be successful and would have to bury many of his mistakes.

> *The Bible contains more true sublimity, more exquisite beauty, more pure morality, more important history, and finer strains of poetry and eloquence, than can be collected from all other books, in whatever age or language they may have been written.*
>
> —SIR WILLIAM JONES

The right attitude plus the right skill makes a substantial difference. When you add to that the right philosophy, namely, that you can have everything in life you want if you will just help enough other people get what they want, which turns things from being self-centered to a secularized version of the golden rule, then success draws ever closer.

To this you must add the right direction. You must have a balanced goals program that encompasses all areas of life. The final key to the success formula is character because all long-term success is character based. This is true in the home, on the job, and in the community. Success and winning relationships are built on trust, and without character, how can there be trust?

Character also produces endurance and persistence when the going gets tough, and life truly is an endurance race, not a sprint. When you follow this simple formula, which over time has proved to be true, you will discover success in all areas of life because you will have the wherewithal to handle whatever comes your way.

———————————

I live my life by doing right, and that is the wisest thing because it will keep me from limping or stumbling and is leading me to real living. (Prov. 4:11–13)

People Are Important

MANY YEARS AGO I heard a story concerning a Native American who said to a visiting missionary, "I like myself better when I am with you." That is the ultimate compliment. When you make people feel better about themselves, you also feel better about yourself.

An article in *Personnel Journal* offered excellent advice:

> Everyone needs to feel he counts for something. If you recognize that need in dealing with people, you will learn to get along with them. Simply show by your actions that you know the other person is quite a person and watch his response. Lord Chesterfield told his son, "Make the other

The most learned, acute, and diligent student cannot, in the longest life, obtain an entire knowledge of this one volume. The more deeply he works the mine, the richer and more abundant he finds the ore; new light continually beams from this source of heavenly knowledge, to direct the conduct, and illustrate the work of God and the ways of men; and he will at last leave the world confessing, that the more he studied the Scriptures, the fuller conviction he had of his own ignorance, and of their inestimable value.

—SIR WALTER SCOTT

person like himself a little bit more and I promise you that he will like you very much indeed." This is one of the most valuable keys to successful human relations. Use it to make additional friends, to get more cooperation, to add magnetism to your personality.

Former insurance executive Walter Hailey adds to this when he advises salespeople to learn about the other person and his business before attempting to make a sale. You will discover something quite fascinating in the process. The more you know about him and his business, the more your prospect will assume that you know how to solve his problems. Not only that, but he will think you are especially nice and very bright indeed.

I will never forget Your words for they are my only hope, so I will keep on obeying You forever and ever, for I am free within the limits of Your laws. (Ps. 119:43–45)

Week Sixteen

There Are Some Moral Absolutes

SOME THINGS are just flat wrong, some are absolutely right, and everything is not relative. For example, I travel a lot, so I'm away from home many nights. Thus far, my wife has never asked me if I had been "relatively" faithful in my absence.

In this age of "relativity," however, many people suffer from the illusion that tolerance and relativity are the ways to go. Dr. Josh McDowell says that his surveys and studies indicate that our children's views about truth make a difference in their behavior. His data prove that when our children do not accept an objective standard of truth, they are 48 percent more likely to cheat on exams, two times more likely to watch a pornographic film, two times more likely to steal, three times more likely to use illegal drugs, six times more likely to attempt suicide, two times more

> So great is my veneration of the Bible, that the earlier my children begin to read it the more confident will be my hope that they will prove useful citizens of their country and respectable members of society.
> —JOHN QUINCY ADAMS

likely to be angry with life, two times more likely to be lacking purpose, and two times more likely to be resentful.

Just as the compass gives us true north and the international time standards set exactness for time, there are truths that can be taught to our children that will benefit them throughout their lives. Admittedly, lying, cheating, and stealing bring certain temporary advantages. Yet when trust is destroyed—as it ultimately will be—the future of the individual who cannot be trusted is limited.

Some parents hide behind the old saw that they love their children too much to deny them anything. They're saying, "I'm not willing to risk finding out just how much authority I have and just how much my child loves me." Ironically, when there is divorce in the family, the child given the choice will generally go with the parent who is more of a loving disciplinarian because children instinctively know their long-range best interests are served when absolutes are established.

Message: Parents, love your kids enough to do what is best for them.

God my Father and Christ Jesus my Lord shower me with kindness, mercy, and peace [God's promise], and I pray for others constantly [my responsibility]. (2 Tim. 1:2–3)

The Rich Are Different from the Poor

ROBERT KIYOSAKI was raised by two dads, one rich, one poor. In his book *Rich Dad, Poor Dad*, written with Sharon L. Lechter, Robert explained the difference in their philosophies. Poor dad: "The love of money is the root of all evil." Rich dad: "The lack of money is the root of all evil." Poor dad: "I can't afford it." Rich dad: "How can I afford it?" Poor dad: "The rich should pay more in taxes to take care of those less fortunate." Rich dad: "Taxes punish those who produce and reward those who don't produce." Poor dad: "Study hard so you can find a good company to work for." Rich dad: "Study hard so you can find a good company to buy." Poor dad: "The reason I'm not rich is because I have you kids." Rich dad: "The reason I must be rich is because I have you kids." Poor dad: "I'll never be rich." Rich dad: "I'm a rich man and rich men don't do this," and "There is a difference between being poor and being broke. Broke is temporary and poor is eternal." Poor dad: "I'm not interested in money," or "Money doesn't matter." Rich dad: "Money is power."

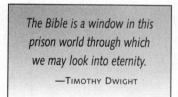

> The Bible is a window in this prison world through which we may look into eternity.
>
> —TIMOTHY DWIGHT

Poor dad wanted Robert to study to become a professional, get a good job, and work for money. Rich dad encouraged him to study, understand how money works, and learn to make it work for him. Rich dad: "Saying 'I can't afford it' makes your brain stop working; asking 'how can I afford it?' puts your brain to work," and saying "I can't afford it" is a sign of mental laziness.

Poor dad was highly educated and intelligent. Rich dad never finished the eighth grade. Both dads earned lots of money. One died leaving tens of millions of dollars to his family, charities, and his church; the other left bills to be paid by his family.

The difference? Their financial philosophies.

I prosper because I am diligent. (Prov. 13:4)

The Splendid Splinter

THAT WAS the nickname given to Ted Williams by newspaper writers, fans, managers, and the public at large. Tall and slender with incredible power, Williams had a long and illustrious career but unfortunately lost three years at his peak as he went off to fight in World War II.

Williams was a quiet individual with lots of pride and determination. He was the last major-league player to hit over .400 when he batted .406 in 1941 and closed out a brilliant career by hitting a home run in his final time at bat.

Ted Williams was a man of integrity. The year before his final year, Ted had the worst season of his career. He was suffering from a pinched nerve in his neck, and it hampered him in the field and at bat. He

> Priests, atheists, skeptics, devotees, agnostics and evangelists are generally agreed that the Authorized Version of the English Bible is the best example of English literature that the world has ever seen.
> —WILLIAM LYON PHELPS

said little about it during the season, but later he explained that the pain was so intense, he could hardly turn his head to look at the pitcher. That year was the first time Ted Williams ever batted under .300, hitting just .254 with ten home runs. At that time he was the highest-salaried player in professional sports, making $125,000 a year. The next year his team, the Boston Red Sox, sent him the same contract for $125,000. He sent it back with a note saying he would not sign it until they gave him the full pay cut allowed. Williams said, "I was always treated fairly by the Red Sox when it came to contracts. Now they were offering me a contract I didn't deserve and I only wanted what I deserved." He cut his own salary by 25 percent. The next year he raised his batting average 62 points and closed out his brilliant career in a blaze of glory.

What Ted Williams did is almost unheard of, but when a person's integrity is at stake, doing the right thing is always the best thing. That approach, over the long haul, will always make you a winner.

I exalt wisdom and wisdom is exalting me. I hold wisdom fast [my responsibility], and she is leading me to great honor and will place a beautiful crown on my head [God's promise]. (Prov. 4:8–9)

The Want-to-Do's vs. The Got-to-Do's

THE MOST COMMON refrain in the media, in private conversations, and in correspondence is this: "I apologize for not getting back sooner, but I've been so busy."

Are we really busier than we've ever been? In reality, based on what ten thousand people recorded in their hour-by-hour time diaries, Americans, on the average, have forty hours a week of discretionary time that we can invest as we please. This is more than we had thirty years ago and five hours more than we had in 1975.

We have so many options of ways to spend our leisure time that we jump from one activity to another, never spending any significant

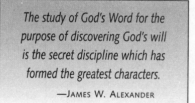

> The study of God's Word for the purpose of discovering God's will is the secret discipline which has formed the greatest characters.
>
> —JAMES W. ALEXANDER

amount of time doing the one thing that would actually bring us more enjoyment. Combine that with the importance placed on leisure time. A poll reported in *U.S. News & World Report* showed that 49 percent of Americans (versus 28 percent in 1986) believe that society needs to stop emphasizing work and put more value on free time.

I'm convinced that much of this feeling has to do with the loss of the ability to concentrate on what we're doing. When they're on the job, many people spend too much time thinking about their home life, and when they're at home, they spend too much time thinking about their jobs.

It's impossible to completely focus on the job for eight hours; your mind naturally moves to other things. But you need to keep the main thing the main thing, and while you're at work, your work is the main thing. When you're at home, family is the main thing. Over a period of time you can bring your thought life under control, which enables you to be more effective on the job and happier at home. That's a good combination, and it's a good approach to take.

———————————————

Jehovah God is my light and protector. He gives me grace and glory and holds no good thing from me [God's promise]. I walk along His paths and am blessed because I trust in Him [my responsibility]. (Ps. 84:11–12)

If I Had to Do It All Over Again . . .

THIS QUESTION is frequently asked of people after they've reached a certain age. One unknown father gave the question serious thought and came up with some answers I believe have a lot of merit:

1. "I would love my wife more in front of my children." That is, he would speak more words of affection, hold her hand more, put his arm around her more, and hug her more.

2. "I would laugh with my children more at our mistakes and joys." Laughter breeds happiness, and a happy home has far fewer problems.

> Don't leave your Bible on the shelf,
> Where days will take their toll
> Of dust and mold and mildew,
> On your poor neglected soul.
>
> —WINNIE ANDREWS

3. "I would listen more, even to the smallest child." It is amazing what little ones can teach us as the pearls of wisdom often come tumbling out.

4. "I would be more honest about my own weaknesses and stop pretending perfection." Kids know we are not perfect, and it's comforting to them to know we can acknowledge our humanness.

5. "I would pray differently for my family. Instead of focusing on them, I'd focus on me." After all, that's really where it starts.

6. "I would do more things together with my children." We repeatedly hear about fathers who get too busy to spend precious moments walking, talking, playing, shopping, fishing, and cycling with their children. That's where bonding takes place.

7. "I would be more encouraging and bestow more praise." It is said that encouragement is the fuel of hope, and praise, particularly for effort, brings about even more effort in the future.

8. "When I made a mistake in the way I dealt with my children, I would admit it and ask them to forgive me."

9. "I would pay more attention to little things, deeds and words of love and kindness." When you add up all those little things over a lifetime, they make a huge difference.

10. "I would share God more intimately with my family through ordinary things that happen in a day."

This unknown father has some marvelous lessons for us. Take his approach, and you will have a happier, more fulfilled life.

As a child of God, I guard my affections, for they influence everything else in my life. (Prov. 4:23)

Week Seventeen

Go-Givers Get More

ONE OF THE MOST complimentary things you can say about a person is that he is a go-getter, meaning he approaches tasks or studies with considerable enthusiasm and stays with it until the task or study has been completed. I'm motivated by go-getters, but the go-givers get more. As a matter of fact, the philosophy upon which we have built our business is the concept that "you can have everything in life you want if you will just help enough other people get what they want."

Dr. Elie Wiesel, a Nobel Peace Prize winner, made this observation: "May I share with you one of the principles that govern my life? It is the realization that what I receive I must pass on to others. The knowledge that I have acquired must not remain imprisoned in my brain. I owe it

> God's Word has been a hammer for nineteen centuries. When other hammers try to break God's eternal anvil of truth, we remember the inscription on the monument to the Huguenots at Paris: "Hammer away, ye hostile hands; Your hammers break; God's anvil stands."
> —SAMUEL ZWEMER

to many men and women to do something with it. I feel that I need to pay back what was given to me. Call it 'gratitude.'"

Most of us want to leave this place better than it was when we arrived. We can do that by teaching our children how to work, how to play, how to live, how to worship our God, how to genuinely love our neighbors, and how to clean up what we've messed up.

We occasionally get complacent, take things for granted, or deny that we have any responsibility to pass on what we have received. That's unfortunate because it has been demonstrated that those who do for others are happier than the recipients of the good deed. Be generous with others, and you will benefit. It's more than just a cliché to say that when you go out looking for friends, you will discover that they are hard to find, but when you go out to be a friend, you will find them everywhere.

I pray for others, and my heart is full of joy because I am making known the good news about Jesus Christ. God continues to help me grow in His grace. (Phil. 1:4–6)

Scouting Teaches Valuable Lessons

A SIGNIFICANT HONOR for me has been election for the fourth time to the National Board of Advisors of the Boy Scouts of America. On the celebration of the eighty-fifth anniversary the Scouts' publication featured the slogan: "Do a good turn daily." Good turns are helpful acts of kindness, done quietly, without boasting, and without expecting a reward or pay. The beauty of the good turn is that it has a positive impact on both the doer and the recipient. Neither one is quite the same afterward.

In wartime Scouts have mobilized to sell war bonds, collect clothing and scrap metal, help harvest crops and plant victory gardens, just to name a few examples. In peacetime Scouts have conducted get-out-the-vote campaigns, collected clothing for refugees, recruited blood donors, and participated in thousands of conservation projects. In recent years the Scouting for Food National Good Turn resulted in the collection of more than 300 million cans of food to help

> We have adopted the convenient theory that the Bible is a Book to be explained, whereas first and foremost it is a Book to be believed . . . There is a world of difference between knowing the Word of God and knowing the God of the Word.
> —LEONARD RAVENHILL

feed more than 20 million hungry Americans, including 5.5 million children.

Conservation has been a theme of Scouting and the inspiration of thousands of Good Turn projects ever since the Boy Scouts of America was established in 1910. The success of Scouts in the business world, as well as in the financial and political worlds, has been well documented. I'm convinced that all parents, particularly single mothers, would do well to encourage their kids to get into Scouting, so their sons and daughters can have appropriate role models. In Scouting the youngsters learn how to work with, cooperate with, and get along with other youngsters their own age. It's marvelous training for the future.

Let's all get behind the Scouting movement in America. Scouts are "gangs" where your son or daughter will enjoy and learn valuable lessons.

I live as a Christian should and stand side by side with the saints, telling the good news without fear, which is a good sign that God is with me. (Phil. 1:27-28)

Progress

MY FAMILY and I went back to Yazoo City, Mississippi, for a family reunion. While I was there, I read both local papers, the *Yazoo City Herald* and the *Jackson Clarion-Ledger*. I was intrigued, saddened, and encouraged about what I read. It was the thirty-fifth anniversary of Governor Ross Barnett's stand in an admissions office doorway to refuse James Meredith admission to the University of Mississippi, resulting in a campus riot that left 2 people dead, 175 injured, and 212 arrested as federal troops restored order.

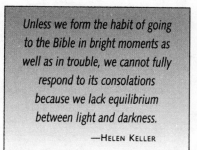

Unless we form the habit of going to the Bible in bright moments as well as in trouble, we cannot fully respond to its consolations because we lack equilibrium between light and darkness.

—HELEN KELLER

Now fast-forward a few years later when Robert J. "Ben" Williams enrolled at the University of Mississippi and went on to achieve significant honors. First, he was welcomed aboard; second, he was the first black football player at Ole Miss, and as a defensive lineman from 1972 to 1975, he made the All-Southeastern Conference team for three years. He was affectionately dubbed "Gentle Ben" and in 1975 was the first black to be given the designation "Colonel Reb" by the student body. That's the highest honor students bestow on a fellow male student. Later he distinguished himself with the Buffalo Bills for nine years as an outstanding defensive lineman.

Since I'm from Yazoo City, as is Gentle Ben, I was particularly thrilled with the progress we made in those years. Fortunately, progress is still being made, and I believe in the years ahead that racism will have died the death it deserves to die. It won't be easy and it will take more years, but as I travel the country, I see many things that encourage me a great deal. This quote from Tim Moody is one of them: "The virtue of angels is that they cannot deteriorate. Their vice is they cannot improve. The vice of people is that their virtue can deteriorate. The virtue of people is that their virtue can also improve."

I let others follow the way I teach and live. I am a pattern for them in my love, faith, and clean thoughts. (1 Tim. 4:12)

An Unlikely Story

HIS NAME IS Gabriel Hjerstedt (YER-stet), and he participated in the 1998 Masters Tournament in Augusta, Georgia. His route to the Masters was one that no Hollywood writer could have created. He is a good golfer, who won the B.C. Open in 1997. But his story is unusual because he had difficulties very few people would be able to overcome.

In 1995 he had to leave the European PGA Tour because he had undiagnosed problems with his jaw that led to panic attacks and depression. Once during a meal in Italy, he experienced cramping in his throat and was rushed to a hospital. Tests could find no cause, but

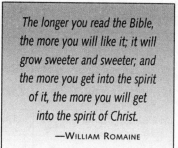

The longer you read the Bible, the more you will like it; it will grow sweeter and sweeter; and the more you get into the spirit of it, the more you will get into the spirit of Christ.
—WILLIAM ROMAINE

the problem persisted for many months. He was so frightened, he was unable to practice even on the driving range. As a result, he hit rock bottom, ran out of money, and slept in his car at gas stations. He was homeless, depressed, and too afraid and too proud to ask for help. The following year a dentist diagnosed a dislocated temporomandibular joint, a dysfunction of the lower jaw, and surgery solved the problem.

Apparently all of these difficulties, combined with persistence and determination, have made him strong and put his game back together. Winning the B.C. Open qualified him for a spot in the prestigious Masters Tournament.

What are the odds of a homeless, depressed man with serious emotional and physical problems making that tournament? He gives all of us hope that we can overcome the odds we face in life and accomplish some marvelous things.

I listen to God, and He has poured out the spirit of wisdom on me and made me wise. (Prov. 1:23)

A Father's Love

FOR FOUR LONG YEARS Jaime Torres Sr. sought the men who shot and killed his nineteen-year-old son, Jaime Torres Jr., in an East Dallas apartment in 1993.

After a time, the trail grew cold and police backed off, but this father never did. A machinery operator from the suburb of Mesquite, he methodically collected the names of witnesses, questioned his relatives, and traveled to Mexico to conduct interviews. His detective work led Chicago police to arrest one suspect who was being held at the Cook County jail and fought extradition to Texas. In October of 1997, information supplied by Torres led Mexican officials to arrest the second suspect in Durango.

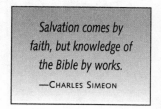

Salvation comes by faith, but knowledge of the Bible by works.
—CHARLES SIMEON

Authorities credited Torres with the arrests. One of the officers said, "You got a father of a deceased victim not letting this go the normal way. He pushed it." Torres stated that he would finally have some peace and he was going to take it easy.

It's not clear what started the argument that led to Jaime Torres's death on June 11, 1993, but the altercation ended in a shoot-out. Jaime was shot five times and died shortly afterward at Parkland Hospital. Torres said, "I don't know how this happened. Sometimes I feel angry, sometimes I feel sad. My body changed, my mind changed. I almost had a heart attack. I lost control." But he said working on the case helped him deal with his grief.

A father's love is a powerful stimulant to see that justice is done, and let's hope that justice was done.

Character communicates the size of the heart and the depth of the soul. You cannot fake authenticity.

———————————

I give thanks to the Lord, for He is good, and His loving-kindness is forever. (Ps. 118:29)

Week Eighteen

That's Not Fair

I'M COMFORTABLE in saying that anyone who has ever done anything of significance has been, at one time or another, unfairly criticized by those who believe they deserve a reward for finding fault. How do you handle unfair, unjust, erroneous criticism?

One effective way is to understand that even the innocent cannot make everyone they encounter a satisfied customer, a cured patient, a happy member of the organization, or a true friend. Not because of what they do or don't do, but because all people have their own faults—including the critics, particularly those who are unfair in their comments.

> The study of God's Word for the purpose of discovering God's will is the greatest discipline which has formed the greatest character.
>
> —ANONYMOUS

Ask for grace to differ from each other in love, especially when you believe that your adversary is wrong. A Jewish scholar of long ago said, "With me it is a very small thing that I should be judged by you or by any human court. I do not even judge myself—it is God who judges me."

A famous American, Dr. Edward Everett, also gives wise counsel. When a newspaper had published false and misleading accounts concerning a certain man, the man went to Dr. Everett for advice. After listening patiently to the man's complaints, Everett said, "My dear sir, do nothing. Half the people who buy that paper never saw the article about you. Half the people who did see it failed to read it. Half of those who read it failed to understand it. Half of those who understood it knew you and refused to believe it. Half of those who believed it were people of no consequence anyway."

To the wisdom of Dr. Everett, add what Stanley Jones said when he called his critics "the unpaid guardians of my soul," and you have an effective method of dealing with your critics.

I humble myself under the mighty hand of God and know that in His time God will lift me up. (1 Peter 5:6)

The Cause of Stress

MANY COMPANIES have long contended that stress in the home causes productivity loss in the marketplace—and it does. But research now reveals that stress on the job causes stress at home. In other words, they feed off each other.

More than ever, remaining competitive is an ongoing challenge. How do we increase productivity and reduce stress in both places?

The solution begins with sensitivity. Research indicates that workers have three prime needs: being involved in interesting work, being recognized for doing a good job, and being let in on what is going on in the company. By looking at these three things, you'll discover that the workers are saying, "Treat me like a person, a human being, not like a number on the payroll. Make me feel important, and when you do, you'll discover that I will be a more relaxed, happier employee. As a result, my productivity will go up. My sick days from stress and stress-induced illness

> *Devout meditation on the Word is more important to soul-health even than prayer. It is more needful for you to hear God's words than that God should hear yours, though the one will always lead to the other.*
>
> —F. B. MEYER

will decline. When all of those things happen, I will arrive home at the end of the day a more contented individual, more apt to function well as a mate or parent, and handle my personal responsibilities with more efficiency."

What all this really means is that the individual will have a better balance in his life. A balanced life reduces stress. Feelings of guilt, which accompany failure either at home or on the job, will be reduced. Let's make others feel important, whether on the job or at home.

I use the special abilities God has given me to help others, passing on to them God's many blessings. (1 Peter 4:10)

This Makes Sense

A STUDENT FLUNKED every course in college before he was kicked out. A few years later one of his professors was astonished at his tremendous financial success and inquired how it happened. The "kicked-out" one responded, "I discovered that if I bought something for one dollar and sold it for three dollars, the profit would add up in a hurry."

In a distorted sense, that's understandable—just as it makes sense to me that the permanent solution to the Social Security issue is to give each individual freedom to use a portion of his Social Security (it's really financial security) funds to invest in the marketplace as they do in Chile. Today, Chile has a vibrant democracy, a very high savings rate, a long string of budget surpluses, high and sustained economic growth, low inflation, and low unemployment. In addition, the country has a wonderfully successful public pension system.

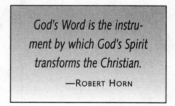

God's Word is the instrument by which God's Spirit transforms the Christian.
—ROBERT HORN

Until 1981, according to an editorial in the *Dallas Morning News* by Timothy O'Leary, Chile's system was much like our Social Security—namely, a pay-as-you-go system in which retirees collect pensions from taxes paid by workers. Chile noticed that its system, like ours, was unsustainable, so it gave workers a choice: stick with the old system, or pay into a new one, investing in state-approved stock funds. Ninety percent of the Chilean workers opted for the new system, with spectacular results. The funds contain $30 billion, an amount equal to roughly 43 percent of Chile's gross domestic product, and the average return has been a whopping 12 percent per year. Benefits are already 50 to 100 percent higher than they would have been under the old system. Retirees are receiving benefits equal to about 80 percent of their average annual income during their last ten years of work. That's almost double the percentage available to U.S. retirees.

My God-given wisdom provides me with a long, good life, riches, honor, pleasure, and peace. (Prov. 13:16–17)

English Is a Tough Language

AROUND THE WORLD it's acknowledged that English, Japanese, and Navajo are three of the toughest languages to learn. Since English is the most popular and is used by more people than any other language in the world, we need to explore why it is so difficult. It is filled with apparent contradictions or oxymorons such as *jumbo shrimp* and *the same difference*. In addition, some local expressions will give you a better understanding of why newcomers to the language may become confused: "It cost him an arm and a leg to get his car fixed"; "Each person coughed up a dollar"; "She was down in the dumps all day"; "The price goes up every time I turn around"; "His eyes popped out when he saw the bill"; "My grandmother has a green thumb"; and "He quit smoking cold turkey."

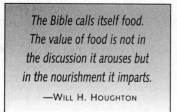

The Bible calls itself food. The value of food is not in the discussion it arouses but in the nourishment it imparts.

—WILL H. HOUGHTON

Then you look at a stack of *wood* and wonder what you *would* do with it. We frequently call a six-foot-six person "Shorty," an overweight person "Skinny," identify some people as "dogs" and then talk about "a dog's life" when many dogs have it much better than some people. We have a tendency to call all black people

"African-Americans" when they could well be Haitians or third-generation Englishmen.

Despite all these puzzling expressions and inconsistencies, those who use English well have a much better chance of winning friends, influencing people, and getting ahead in life. Learn your English, but in the process please understand that America is one of the very few nations on the globe that do not require its students to learn another language. If an immigrant struggles with our language, we need to ask ourselves, How much of his language do we know? It's something to think about, isn't it?

One publication speaks clearly and frankly. It's the Holy Bible. You have probably noticed that God did not call the Ten Commandments "the Ten Suggestions."

God will never forsake me because I trust in Him. (Ps. 9:10)

Frustrated Housewife + Impatient Husband = Successful Business

ONE SUNDAY EVENING, way back in 1927 in Fremont, Michigan, a young man named Dan was waiting impatiently for his wife to feed their seven-month-old daughter. They had a social commitment, and Dan didn't want to be late. He paced back and forth, looking at his watch without saying anything, nevertheless indicating that he was anxious to go. In the meantime, his wife, Dorothy, was straining vegetables into a bowl piece by piece.

After a time his patience ran thin, and he stomped into the kitchen, pleading with his wife to hurry up. That's when Dorothy decided to teach Dan a lesson. "To press the point," Dorothy later recalled, "I dumped a whole container of peas into a strainer and bowl, placed them in Dan's lap, and asked him to see how he'd like to do that three times a day, seven days a week."

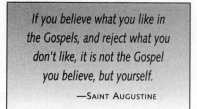

If you believe what you like in the Gospels, and reject what you don't like, it is not the Gospel you believe, but yourself.

—SAINT AUGUSTINE

Dan got Dorothy's message and decided to do something about it. The next day in his family-owned cannery, he developed an idea to put something different in the cans: strained baby food. That first year they sold 590,000 cans of Gerber's baby food at 15 cents per can, helped establish the baby food market, and dominated that market for several decades.

When you're frustrated and irritated about a never-ending problem, the logical thing to do is ask, Does this problem have a solution, and if so, what is it? That's the process Dan Gerber went through, and when he came up with a solution, he became a hero to millions of mothers throughout the world. The Gerber family and millions of mothers have benefited enormously as a result.

I'm delighted when the Lord chastens and corrects me because it proves that I am His child and that He delights in making me better. (Prov. 3:11–12)

Week Nineteen

One Hundred Years Young and Still Going Strong

Lois Lacy Lewis of Greenville, Texas, celebrated her one-hundredth birthday and claimed it "nearly killed her," but she said it with a smile. About three hundred relatives, neighbors, and friends showed up for the celebration. She got a congratulatory card from the White House, and Willard Scott mentioned her on the *Today Show*.

> The doctrines of the Bible are all practical and its laws all reasonable. Every doctrine has its practical therefore and every law its doctrinal because.
>
> —John Brown

Mrs. Lewis started her career as an elementary school teacher in 1916, and for nearly half a century she worked in education. She married, raised three children, and earned her bachelor's and master's degrees from East Texas State Teachers College. Her husband died in 1966 after a long illness.

In 1960 her career as a columnist started at the *Celeste Courier*, now the *Leonard Graphic*. This paper in Greenville has a circulation of about 1,100, and many people said they read it just to see what Mrs. Lewis was going to write about. She amazed every one with her memory and her local community resources. Her column, "Mrs. Lewis Writes," focused on the Celeste population of 973, which bills itself as "a small town with a big heart." Each week she wrote her column in blue ink on a yellow notepad and sent it in a stamped, self-addressed envelope to the *Graphic*.

In 1990, Mrs. Lewis sold her house in Celeste and moved into a retirement home in Greenville. She continued to write her column, was an active member of the Methodist church in Celeste, and belonged to the Coffee Club, a local group that met weekly at the First National Bank of Celeste, until she passed away in November of 1998 at the age of 101.

Mrs. Lewis's story inspired me because some people think they're old at sixty. She was young at heart and still making a contribution at one hundred and one.

I love Your laws and have great peace of heart and mind and do not stumble. (Ps. 119:165)

Work Is No Joke

HERE IS ONE of my favorite quips about work: Someone asked a worker how long he had been working for his company, and he smilingly responded, "Ever since they threatened to fire me." We read numerous articles about people complaining about the workload. However, *USA Today* reported in the April 7, 1998, issue that 52 percent of those who said they had too much work to do expressed satisfaction with their jobs. In all fairness, 65 percent of those who felt their workload was about right expressed satisfaction with their jobs.

Only 45 percent of those who felt they had too little or much too little to do expressed satisfaction with their jobs. To me, that is an interesting bit of information because a common belief is that many people want to do as little as they can and yet get paid as much as possible. The latter part is undoubtedly true, but the survey shows that nearly half of workers without enough to do are not satisfied with their jobs. Some dissatisfaction accompanies the knowledge that time, talent, and abilities are not being properly used.

> *The religion in which our Lord was brought up was first and foremost a religion of subjection to the authority of a written divine Word.*
>
> —J. I. PACKER

Very few things are as satisfying as being able to say to yourself, "Today was a good day. I did my job and a little extra. I feel good about that, and I feel good about myself." A productive employee who is kept busy working at his job is far more likely to be happy at that job and less likely to look for employment elsewhere. That's why it is important that workers are gainfully employed while they're on the job. Being productive gives people a sense of satisfaction and fulfillment that loafing never can.

I accept with gratitude the forgiveness Christ extends to me, which covers all of my sins, since I have never blasphemed the Holy Spirit. (Mark 3:28-29)

If He Can, You Can

KACEY MCCALLISTER lives in Keizer, a suburb of Salem, Oregon. He plays basketball, and in baseball he has been catcher and covered positions at first base and in the outfield. His play was so spectacular that a Little League team in North Carolina dedicated its season to him, and disabled Boy Scouts in Georgia were inspired by him. People all over America have been inspired by Kacey, who lost both legs at the hip when he was run over by a truck a few years ago.

He does all of those things by propelling himself with his arms. He has a tremendous attitude and a determination to live as any other youngster wants to live, and the nation is applauding him. CNN sent a crew to the family's home to do a story on him. Kacey said he was more motivated than ever: "I want to show them that I really can do all this stuff."

> ## The Bible
>
> *It is God's highway to Paradise.*
> *It is the light on the pathway in the darkest night.*
> *It leads business men to integrity and uprightness.*
> *It is the great consoler in bereavement.*
> *It awakens men and women opiated by sin.*
> *It answers every great question of the soul.*
> *It solves every great problem of life.*
>
> —A. Z. CONRAD

In today's world when too many people complain about everything, here's a role model who is determined to make the most of life. Where do his drive, commitment, and enthusiasm for life come from? I suspect his mother and father are much of the source of his inspiration. Instead of spoiling him by catering to his whims and allowing him to feel sorry for himself, they've made the wise choice of encouraging him to believe in himself and letting him do everything he can do, while still being available to help when it is required. That's love in action, and the results are spectacular.

I am sure I belong to Christ because I do what He wants me to do.
(1 John 2:3)

It's the Economy, Stupid!

PRESIDENT CLINTON was elected in 1992 after a campaign built largely around the phrase, "It's the economy, stupid!" Today the campaign slogan should be, "It's integrity, stupid!"

Many believe that if the economy is fine, character does not matter, but others have observed that if the economy goes south, the character issue will be magnified a thousandfold.

When I was a youngster in Yazoo City, Mississippi, I worked in a grocery store. One day I overheard a man make a proposal to the owner of the store that sounded wonderfully good to me. As a youngster, I couldn't understand why the boss did not immediately accept the offer. When the man left, I asked my boss why he didn't take advantage of that opportunity. His answer was sobering: "You can't make a good deal with a bad guy."

> Prayer is the "open sesame" of the Bible. Always begin your Bible reading with prayer for divine guidance. All of us in reading some current book have wished the author were present to answer and explain some things, but this is rarely possible. Amazing as it seems, this is possible when reading the Bible.
>
> —G. S.

The person who doesn't believe that character counts has

never talked to a wife whose husband has walked out on her, leaving her with three small children to raise and no job skills to provide meaningful income. Nor has he talked with a husband whose wife chose to run off with another man. The individual who says character doesn't count has not talked to one of the hundreds of business owners who go bankrupt each year because of employee theft.

John Wooden, the legendary basketball coach of the UCLA Bruins, who set records that undoubtedly will never be broken, said he was concerned about what the athletes did at practice but far more concerned about what they did between today's practice and tomorrow's practice. He contended that what one does off the job determines how far he goes on the job. He was talking about character, and he's right.

I love my Christian brothers because, although I have never yet seen God, when I love others God lives in me and His love is more fully expressed. (1 John 4:11–12)

What's Going On?

NUMEROUS CONTRADICTIONS are apparent in our society. We are inundated with statistics proving that crime is decreasing, the economy is better than ever, unemployment is at a thirty-year low, and technology is solving many problems. Yet we are also being told that there are more poor people than there were twenty or thirty years ago. Newspapers and TV news shows

---

The Bible

Century follows century—There it stands.
Empires rise and fall and are forgotten—There it stands.
Dynasty succeeds dynasty—There it stands.
Kings are crowned and uncrowned—There it stands.
Emperors decree its extermination—There it stands.
Despised and torn to pieces—There it stands.
Storms of hate swirl about it—There it stands.
Atheists rail against it—There it stands.
Agnostics smile cynically—There it stands.
Profane prayerless punsters caricature it—There it stands.
Unbelief abandons it—There it stands.

—A. Z. CONRAD

---

report tragedy after tragedy—school shootings across the nation and countless other examples.

What's going on? Since belief determines behavior, doesn't it make sense that we should be teaching ethical, moral values in every home and in every school in America? Unfortunately, much of the media and music glorifies violence and gratuitous sex with no serious consequences. In essence that's what we are being taught to believe.

I wonder what would have happened in the schools where fatal shootings occurred had the Ten Commandments been posted and read to the students at least once a month throughout their academic experience? I'm convinced that alone would have dramatically reduced the possibilities of those teens getting weapons of destruction and gunning down helpless, innocent people.

For those who say that character doesn't count, I challenge you to ask any of the families of the victims of those school shootings. It would take a lot of doing to get those Ten Commandments posted in our schools, but there is nothing preventing them from being taught and modeled at home repeatedly and consistently.

I have received the Holy Spirit, and He lives within my heart, so I don't need anyone to teach me what is right. He teaches me all things. (1 John 2:27)

Week Twenty

Against All Odds

JEFFREY PARDEE is an enthusiastic, highly motivated young athlete who has lived virtually all of his life with pain. When he was eighteen months old, he started having trouble with his hands, and by the time he was eight, he had undergone surgery and become a regular patient at Texas Scottish Rite Hospital. His problems aren't confined to his hands; he also suffers from migraine headaches and major muscle weaknesses in his back. His mother says, "He has a muscle system out of whack."

The young man plays basketball, baseball, and soccer; is an honor student at Larson Academy; plays in the school orchestra; and sings in the choir. In addition, he is a champion swimmer with ribbons from the Pan American Games to prove it. According to *Rite Up*, the 1998 Spring bulletin of the Scottish Rite Hospital for Children, Jeffrey swims at least five days a week and sometimes trains both before and after school.

> *All the distinctive features and superiority of our republican institutions are derived from the teachings of Scripture.*
> —EDWARD EVERETT

The pain is constant and sometimes those muscles won't quite cooperate, but "his spirit is as buoyant as a float bouncing on top of the water."

Jeffrey is training harder than ever to reach his next goal, which is to someday swim in the Olympics. With his commitment, determination, and optimistic attitude, don't be surprised if you see him representing the United States on the Olympic swim team.

Much credit obviously goes to his family, and it's wonderful that the Scottish Rite Hospital, without charging a dime, can work a miracle with Jeffrey. He's had lots of encouragement, but he's the kind of young man who delights in encouraging and helping others. Jeffrey—along with all of those wonderful people at the Scottish Rite Hospital—has a new lease on life.

I always remember to be loyal and kind. I hold these virtues tightly and have written them deep within my heart. (Prov. 3:3)

This, Too, Shall Pass

THE GOOD NEWS is that unemployment in America is at one of its lowest points in history. Everyone who has a financial interest in survival and doing well is excited about that. But there is another side to the coin. Many in the service business, particularly in the restaurant industry, are having difficulty getting and keeping good employees. As a result, the service in restaurants is declining, with the exception of the well-established restaurants that have employees who do well financially and who are treated with respect.

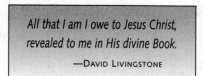

All that I am I owe to Jesus Christ, revealed to me in His divine Book.
—DAVID LIVINGSTONE

How do we take this situation and make it a win-win-win for the employer, employee, and customer? First, remember that when employees are well trained, confident in what they are doing, and learning new things on a regular basis, they are far less likely to leave their jobs. Research conclusively proves that people stay where they grow. Personal growth increases excitement and has a direct impact on their attitude, and they, in turn, positively affect the attitudes of the other employees.

Second, express appreciation for a job well done. The Department of Labor reports that 46 percent of the people who voluntarily leave their jobs do so because they do not feel appreciated. A sincere "thank you" works wonders.

Third, set the example. Be a good role model. Consistently do what you want your employees to do (be courteous, prompt, dependable, etc.), and avoid doing what you don't want them to do on the job (smoke, have a sloppy appearance, use foul language, gossip, exhibit sexist or racist behavior, etc.). It is still true that example is the best teacher, and if you set the example you won't have to set the rule.

Train them; praise them; model for them. Doing these things will give you, your employees, and your customers a better chance in life.

I have received wealth from the Lord, along with the good health to enjoy it. (Eccl. 5:19)

Good News—You Can Change!

IN THE WORLDS of education, athletics, business, and government, it's recognized that a person's attitude is often the determining factor in how well he does. In the business world the dominant factor of successful employees identified by employers was attitude.

Unfortunately, there are more people with a negative rather than a positive attitude. Fortunately, however, people can change. Psychologist Shad Helmstetter advised, "You can't change from a negative mindset to a positive mind-set without changing from negative talking to positive talking. To do that, you must change the input from negative to positive."

Here's how. First, make a conscious decision: "Yes, I can change, I am changing, and I will continue to change." Claim that as a positive affirmation, and repeat it to yourself several times each day. Second, seek friends and family who are optimistic and upbeat, and spend more time with them. Third, pick up an optimistic, upbeat, self-help book that gives specific instructions on how to move from the negative to the positive.

> To say nothing of its holiness or authority, the Bible contains more specimens of genius and taste than any other volume in existence.
>
> — WALTER SAUAGUE LANDOR

Fourth, acquire the tapes of a speaker, preacher, or teacher you enjoy and admire whose messages are upbeat and uplifting. Listen to each tape until you can complete many of the sentences, examples, illustrations, and stories. At that point the message becomes positive self-talk, and over a period of time you will change from the negative to the positive. With a new positive mind-set you will have the confidence to acquire the new skills that will make a major difference in your life.

―――――――――――――――――

I follow the steps of the godly and stay on the right path, so I enjoy life to the full. (Prov. 2:20–21)

Quarterback Is the "Glamour" Position

MOST KIDS with the size and athletic ability to play football dream of becoming a quarterback in the National Football League. That was Paul Hornung's dream. After he received the Heisman Trophy playing for Notre Dame, he was drafted in the first round by Green Bay as quarterback. However, Green Bay had a truly great quarterback in Bart Starr, and for the first couple of years Hornung saw limited action. In many regards the first-round draft pick was being wasted because the rookie, as good as he was in college, wasn't about to replace the very successful and capable veteran.

Then along came Vince Lombardi. As the new coach, he watched Hornung carefully and knew that he was big, fast, and tough, and that he was particularly effective once the ball was inside the twenty-yard line.

> The Gospel is not merely a book—it is a living power—a book surpassing all others. I never omit to read it, and every day with the same pleasure. Nowhere is to be found such a series of beautiful ideas, and admirable moral maxims, which pass before us like the battalions of a celestial army . . . The soul can never go astray with this book for its guide.
>
> —NAPOLEON ON ST. HELENA

When the chips were down, he was the "go to" guy or "money player" who could get the tough yards when he "smelled" the end zone. Lombardi made Hornung a running back. That's when, in the sixties, the Packers started their string of championships. Hornung went on to become Most Valuable Player and was All-Pro four times. He still holds several records and has been inducted into the Pro Football Hall of Fame.

Paul Hornung didn't make it as a quarterback, but as far as I know, he never complained. He took the hand he was dealt and played it with passion and enthusiasm. That's a winning approach.

My teaching is so correct that anyone who wants to argue will be ashamed of himself because there won't be anything to criticize. (Titus 2:8)

Service Is the Key

AN ISSUE of the Southwest Airlines magazine carried an article about computer magnate Michael Dell, one of the most successful entrepreneurs in our country today. Dell explained the success of his company. He believes he and his employees are successful and will continue to be successful because of their unique relationships with their customers. He stated, "As long as we continue to pay heed to what our customers tell us they want, and deliver products and services that are meaningful to them, and that deliver superior value, we will continue to be successful."

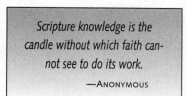

Scripture knowledge is the candle without which faith cannot see to do its work.

—ANONYMOUS

I might point out, this is not a new concept or idea, but too many people and companies have lost the service concept. Many years ago Henry Ford said that if we give truly outstanding service and genuinely care about the people we serve, our profits will be embarrassingly large. Two thousand years ago the Carpenter from Galilee stated, "He who would be the greatest among you must become the servant of all."

When we put the other person's feelings and needs above our own, amazingly enough, our needs will be met big time. People who do the right thing, and often the nice thing, are the ones who are the most successful in their businesses and happier in their personal lives as well.

———————————————

I am called to teach and encourage others, and I do these things with all the strength and energy that God supplies so that God will be glorified through Jesus Christ. (1 Peter 4:11)

Too Much of a Good Thing

FOR SOME strange reason millions of us believe that if a little of something is good for us, a lot would be even better. Sometimes that is true, but frequently it is not. For example, if a nonswimmer has fallen into water over his head, throwing him one end of a rope is good. Throwing him both ends of a rope is bad.

In physical fitness, many people believe that if jogging two miles a day is good for them, ten miles would be better. Many people believe that if one dose of a particular medication once a day is good for them, two should be twice as good. Disaster has been the result of that kind of thinking. However, this is not true in all cases. If a little kindness and consideration are good, it's true that a lot would be even better. It's also true that if it is good to read for twenty minutes a day, it could be better to read three times that much, depending on schedule and interests.

> If there be any mistakes in the Bible, there may as well be a thousand. If there be one falsehood in that book, it did not come from the God of truth.
> —JOHN WESLEY

Common sense and expert advice are important. In 1972 I needed to get on a sensible eating and exercise program, so I sought the advice of Dr. Ken Cooper of aerobics fame. He started me on a sound, research-based program. I followed his advice, and now more than a quarter century later, I'm in better shape and my energy level is measurably higher than when I was forty-five years old.

The word that goes jointly with common sense is *balance*. We need to have balance in our lives if we are going to be able to get the maximum amount of enjoyment from them. Think about these things. Take this approach, and you'll have a much better chance of staying up, up, up in a down, down world.

I try to live in such a way so that no one will ever be offended or fail to find the Lord by the way I act, so that no one can find fault with me and blame it on the Lord. (2 Cor. 6:3)

A Sense of Humor Helps

ANY BASEBALL FAN in America will immediately recognize the fact that Jackie Robinson was the first African-American to play major-league baseball. In college he had been a tremendous three-sport star, excelling in football, baseball, and basketball. When Branch Rickey offered him the opportunity to play in the major leagues, Jackie accepted with excitement and had a long talk with Rickey, who warned him of all the challenges he would have to face in his career.

He cautioned him about being careful to control part of his competitive spirit, particularly the inclination to lose his temper in the heat of competition. He warned Jackie there would be racial slurs and prejudice of all kinds, but he had an opportunity to make history and establish a significant precedent.

A readiness to believe every promise implicitly, to obey every command unhesitatingly, to stand perfect and complete in all the will of God, is the only true spirit of Bible study.

—ANDREW MURRAY

The rest of the story, as the books say, is history. Jackie Robinson went on to become one of baseball's all-time greats and set significant records in the major leagues. What many people do not realize about Jackie Robinson, however, is that he also had a unique sense of humor. On the first day he started with the Dodgers, he kissed his wife good-bye and, with a twinkle in his eye, said, "If you come to the ballpark today, you won't have any trouble recognizing me." He paused for a moment, then added, "My number is 42."

Eventually Jackie Robinson had lots to smile about, but those early months and years were challenging and demanding. He accomplished a major objective and became one of the most respected athletes in major-league history, and in the process he gave millions of fans something to smile about.

God showers down on me the richness of His grace, for He knows and understands me and knows what is best for me at all times. *(Eph. 1:8)*

Manners Matter

MY MOTHER TAUGHT her children that while we might not be the richest people around, we could be courteous, polite, and considerate of others. We were taught to say "please," "thank you," "yes, sir," "yes, ma'am," not to talk with food in our mouths, and a few other little niceties.

Now there are some indications that manners are on the way back "in." In 1996 a survey revealed that 78 percent of Americans believed incivility had gone from bad to worse in the preceding ten years, and many believed it had eroded values and contributed to violence in our society. Today many companies are sponsoring workshops to teach professional etiquette and protocol in the marketplace. Reports abound that job candidates are turned down if they begin eating before their host does and salt food before tasting it because it shows a tendency toward making hasty decisions. Those who order the most expensive items on the menu and conclude with an expensive dessert are generally not offered jobs for fear they will abuse an expense account.

> In the divine Scriptures, there are shallows and there are deeps; shallows where the lamb may wade, and deeps where the elephant may swim.
>
> —JOHN OWEN

Obviously, much of this involves common sense as much as manners, but it really boils down to thinking in terms of what's in the other person's best interests. When we think that way, we act that way, and invariably what's in the other person's best interests from a business perspective turns out to be in our best interests as well.

Studies by Harvard, the Stanford Research Institute, and the Carnegie Foundation suggest that success in a job depends 85 percent on people skills and only 15 percent on technical knowledge and skill. People who have the right attitude and work with others effectively are in the most demand and occupy the higher positions. Message: Use common sense and mind your manners.

I cheer other Christians up and help them. As brothers and sisters in the Lord, we share the same spirit, and my heart is tender and sympathetic. (Phil. 2:1–2)

Advice from Helen

WHEN SHE WAS nineteen months old, Helen Keller was afflicted with a disease that seriously impaired her hearing and destroyed her sight. She observed that every day we should value our sight and use it as if today would be the last day we would be able to see. I wonder how many times we even think about our gift of sight and truly enjoy the beauty of our immediate surroundings, the faces of our mates, children, grandchildren, and friends.

Obviously there are more senses than just that of sight. I have an acquaintance in the insurance business who many years ago, through some unknown cause, awakened one morning profoundly deaf. He wrote that it was difficult to imagine the grief you feel when you realize that you will never again be able to hear your friends and loved ones say, "I love you, and I miss you."

> The Bible is a rock of diamonds, a chain of pearls, the sword of the Spirit; a chart by which the Christian sails to eternity; the map by which he daily walks; the sundial by which he sets his life; the balance in which he weighs his actions.
>
> —THOMAS WATSON

The sense of smell is another of our take-it-for-granted joys. The aroma of a delicious meal cooking or the fragrance of flowers, newly cut grass, a clean, fresh baby, or for me, the perfume my beautiful redheaded wife wears.

This morning, while listening to an audiotape, I heard thoughts expressed by Helen Keller and realized that I generally take all of these things for granted and seldom acknowledge the gifts of seeing, hearing, tasting, touching, smelling, thinking, and feeling. Take a moment to give thanks for your wonderful gifts. You'll feel blessed all day.

I do what I do not for my own profit but because Christ's love controls me. He died for me so that I might have eternal life, so I no longer live for myself, but to please Him. (2 Cor. 5:14–15)

Wisdom's Rewards

YOU WILL NEVER see a vain, conceited, arrogant, egotistical *wise* person. We frequently see vain, conceited, arrogant, egotistical educated and/or knowledgeable people. The reason is clear: arrogance, conceit, and vanity generally come because we've achieved our expertise and knowledge in certain fields of endeavor by the sweat of our brows. We are "self-made," so the ego swells because of what *we* have done, and we often become unbearable.

You will never see a wise person who suffers from these personality disasters because a wise person understands that wisdom is a gift from God. Wisdom, in its simplistic form, is the correct use of the truth in the knowledge you have acquired. Since God has

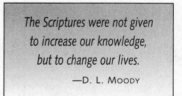

The Scriptures were not given to increase our knowledge, but to change our lives.
—D. L. MOODY

blessed you with wisdom, you have nothing to be vain or conceited about.

Perhaps you have wondered why some people with limited formal education are able to achieve such great success in life. These people are generally wise and either knowingly or unknowingly are following biblical principles. My mother finished only the fifth grade and was widowed during the depression with six children too small to work. She had a limited amount of knowledge, but she was constantly in prayer. God answered her prayers and gave her wisdom so that she made excellent decisions.

I am living by the Holy Spirit's power and am following Him in every part of my life, so I don't need to look for honors and popularity, which lead to jealousy and hard feelings. (Gal. 5:25–26)

Week Twenty-Two

Why I Will Succeed

CHARLES SURASKY said some nice things about one of my books and gave me permission to use his comments in a book or column. This writing was produced at the request of the managing partner of a West Coast legal practice and was a significant part of a larger project:

I will succeed because I am a winner

I will succeed because every lesson I've learned has prepared me for this challenge

> *Forgiving means to pardon the unpardonable. Faith means believing the unbelievable. And hoping means to hope when things are hopeless.*
> —G.K. CHESTERTON

I will succeed because I want to succeed and because people believe in me and trust me

I will succeed because success will help me to grow into a bigger and better person

I will succeed because I know what I must do

I will succeed because my family is the foundation of my success

I will succeed because success is the most important legacy
I can bequeath to my children
I will succeed because my wife and I are inseparable,
unstoppable and uniquely talented
I will succeed because I've faced opportunities before and
I have triumphed
I will succeed because success is a birthright I inherited
from my parents and my ancestors
I will succeed because I've always wanted to expand the
range of challenges in my life
I will succeed because I have family, friends and acquain-
tances who want to—and will—help me
I will succeed because I am young, healthy and dynamic
I will succeed because my plan for success is flexible and
my thirst for success is unquenchable
I will succeed

Surasky covered some poignant thoughts, and I noticed that
he included no "if-only's" or "I plan to's" or "I'm a'gonna do's."
If all of us borrowed the concepts identified here, more of us
would experience greater success.

---

*I follow the truth and obey God's command, and He has told me to
love my fellow Christians. I obey God and do whatever He tells me
to do. (2 John 4–6)*

We Do It If We Justify It

MANY PEOPLE are looking for excuses to justify drinking alcohol. However, the *New England Journal of Medicine* in December 1997 completed the largest study ever undertaken on drinking habits and disease rates of nearly 500,000 men and women, ages 30 to 104. The study covered a fifteen-year period and revealed that one drink a day was associated with a 40 percent reduction in the incidence of heart attacks in persons over fifty. However, the study pointed out the downsides of alcohol. It is calorically dense and nutritionally sparse. It puts weight on with few health benefits, and many people don't know when they've had enough. In the real world, only a minority of Americans limit themselves to a single drink. Add smoking to the mix, and you lose all the benefits from the booze— and then some.

> Unless God's Word illumine the way, the whole life of men is wrapped in darkness and mist, so that they cannot but miserably stray.
>
> —JOHN CALVIN

The study emphasized other ways to obtain alcohol's cardiac benefits without the risks. Alcohol protects the heart by raising the level of the good cholesterol, but so do the right diet, exercising, and if necessary, taking a cholesterol-lowering pill. Alcohol protects the heart by reducing the tendency of the blood to form clots, but so does aspirin. Prolonged drinking hurts the liver and brain and is the number one cause of automobile accidents, broken homes, and domestic violence. Drinkers are at greater risk for cirrhosis of the liver, and for cancers of the mouth, esophagus, pharynx, larynx, and liver, so it makes sense to take the alternate route and avoid those infinitely more destructive results that alcohol brings. Avoid alcohol, and you'll find it easier to stay up, up, up in a down, down world.

The truth is in my heart forever, so God the Father and Jesus Christ His Son bless me with great mercy, much peace, truth, and love. (2 John 2–3)

Home, Sweet Home

THE STORY is told of a little girl who was away from home for the first time at camp. At bedtime she was seen with tears streaming down her cheeks, and a camp counselor asked, "Are you homesick?" The little girl replied, "No, I'm not homesick. I'm heresick."

The word *home* is part of everyone's vocabulary, whether he has a home or not. Every time I return from a trip, whether I've been gone a day or several days, I'm always glad to get home. Many times people speak of their place of business as their "home away from home." Periodically someone will leave a place of employment, return later, and make the comment, "Man, I feel like I'm back home!" The same is true of athletes who sometimes make the circuit from one team to another, and yet there is a favorite place that just feels like home.

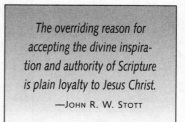

The overriding reason for accepting the divine inspiration and authority of Scripture is plain loyalty to Jesus Christ.
—JOHN R. W. STOTT

Home is used in a lot of statements: "The point hit home," "The batter hit a home run," and "The runner is rounding third and is headed home." Most of the time the word *home* signifies victory, accomplishment, security, peace of mind, and other

217

positive thoughts. Yet there are those who do not have homes, and still others who have places of residence but they're certainly not homes in the sense that most of us think in terms of home. Any number of things can replace the feeling of security associated with home with a feeling of fright and dread—an abusive or addicted parent or an absentee parent. For children who live under those circumstances, encouragement and education play a major role in their future. People with homes that genuinely are havens have much to be grateful for.

I have joy because I have salvation, which comes from God. (Ps. 3:8)

Crime and Illiteracy

AN EXTENSIVE ARTICLE in the May 3, 1998, edition of the *Dallas Morning News* describes a program to fight illiteracy called HOPE, an acronym for Helping Others Pursue Education. It is a program started by Lucy Smith of Hurst, Texas, who trains the volunteer teachers at the Hutchins State Jail in South Dallas County.

Since 85 to 90 percent of inmates in the TDCJ (Texas Department of Criminal Justice) cannot read, and the rate of recidivism is enormously high, this program should reduce recidivism substantially. That's important because a 1 percent reduction in offenders returning to prison can create a savings of $6.6 million, and the two-year HOPE program costs only about $800 per student. That will lead to huge

> It matters not what others do,
> For God has left a standard true,
> I'll search its pages day by day,
> And pray for courage to obey.
>
> —TULLETT

financial savings and, even more important, ensure the futures of the men and women involved.

The inmates who can read are teaching those who cannot read. The confidence and the self-esteem they get from teaching are equaled only by the feelings of confidence and self-esteem the illiterates acquire as they begin to read.

The program is a faith-based one and is completely voluntary, under the direction of the prison chaplain. Senior Warden Elvis Hightower said, "The self-esteem they get is just amazing." Deshoaun Green, the first student to admit his illiteracy aloud, said, "It's a wonderful feeling to look up and read what's on the board and get it, for the first time in my life."

When there is hope in the future, there is power in the present, and since hope is the foundational quality of all change, there is considerable reason to be excited about this program. If this program spreads throughout the state and nation, it will give countless thousands of others hope with believability.

I am protected by Your mercy and Your love, and I worship You with deepest awe. (Ps. 5:7)

Disability or Different Ability?

HANK NICHOLS, who is mentally disabled, has found a warm welcome at St. Francis Episcopal Church. The church is Franciscan spiritually and "takes in everybody." An article by Mary A. Jacobs published in the *Dallas Morning News* spotlighting Hank quotes Elise Mitchell, a member there: "Among people with disabilities, I think those with mental disabilities have the toughest time being accepted. They can't always communicate well." Periodically they are asked to leave a church and are often tolerated but not really accepted.

Nichols runs a one-man campaign for regular attendance. If anyone misses even one Sunday, Hank will call and ask, "Where were you?" Member Ray Pearce Jr. says, "It's very endearing. He cares, and he pays attention."

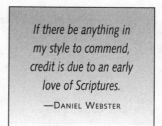

If there be anything in my style to commend, credit is due to an early love of Scriptures.

—DANIEL WEBSTER

For more than twenty years Nichols has held a job with the grounds crew at the University of Texas Southwestern Medical Center. He received an award for punctuality. One morning he was hit by a car, "got up, dusted himself off and got to work on time," says Sister Mary Alice, counselor-trainer at Storey Lane Chateau, an independent living center for mentally disabled adults. He participates in drama, chorale, and swimming at Bachman Therapeutic Center and competes in the Special Olympics. His different ability includes an uncanny gift for remembering numbers. He rattles off the phone numbers of church members and associates without a pause and knows the names and birthdays of each of the church's fifty to sixty children. Church member Tom Pruit confirms, "I have seven children and he knows all their birthdays. He always sends cards and calls on their birthdays." Adult church members ruefully add that Nichols also knows—and often recites—everybody's age.

Yes, Hank has a different ability. But the church is richer and better off because he's there—and so is Hank.

God gives me the good sense to stay away from evil. (Prov. 2:11)

Week Twenty-Three

What About Loyalty?

As ONE of the most colorful managers of all time, Casey Stengel, manager of the New York Yankees for several years, earned a lot of extremely loyal fans. Included on his team were Billy Martin, Whitey Ford, Bobby Richardson, Yogi Berra, Mickey Mantle, and a number of other outstanding players. However, as any coach or manager will tell you, it takes a special talent to convert a team of all-stars into an all-star team.

Casey had that unique ability. He was so good at it that during his stint, he won seven World Series and ten American League pennants. This record was head and shoulders above what any other major-league manager was able to do with his team.

> An honest man with an open Bible and a pad and pencil is sure to find out what is wrong with him very quickly.
>
> —A. W. TOZER

So what was Casey's reward for this incredible record? He got fired. The circumstances are a little unusual, to say the least. When Bill Mazeroski of the Pittsburgh Pirates hit a dramatic bottom-of-the-ninth home run in the seventh and deciding game, the New York Yankees lost the 1960 World Series. Stengel was dumped just five days later and said, "I've been fired because of my age. I'll never make the mistake of being seventy again."

The New York Yankees' owner had the right to do what he did. However, it's like the bull standing on the railroad track. You admire his courage, but you question his judgment. You can admire the people in Yankee management for doing what they thought was right, but you must question their judgment for firing such an incredibly successful manager.

And what about fairness? Doesn't success deserve some kind of loyalty? Casey's fans were terribly upset about that turn of events, and it causes all of us to wonder what we have to do to develop a sense of loyalty on both sides of the table. Loyalty is a very valuable character quality, and those who have it will have friends and fans wherever they go.

Because I have self-control, I control my tongue. (Prov. 13:3)

Decisions in Giving

MY FRIEND Charlie "Tremendous" Jones granted me permission to quote from a letter he sent to his grandchildren.

On giving:

Never give to get, give because you have received. Giving is like a muscle. To be strong you have to exercise it and to grow as a person, giving is the exercise. You can't really enjoy anything without sharing it. This includes your faith, love, talents and money. Someday you'll discover we never really give, we're only returning and sharing a small portion of what we've received.

> *Blame none but yourself if all the Bible you get is that little bit from under the calendar hurriedly snatched as a sop to conscience.*
>
> —DAVID SHEPHERD

On decisions:

The more decisions you make, the more tremendous your life will be. Don't wait for the right time, do something now, today. Don't worry about big decisions, make many little ones and the big ones will seem little. Your job is not to make a right decision as much as to make one and invest your life making it right.

You only have two big decisions in LIFE. Your marriage and your work. Don't look for what you like to do. Find something that needs to be done and prepare to do it. You'll discover the joy of doing something that ought to be done while others are wasting their lives searching for something they would like to do. Don't waste time looking for a better job. Do a better job and you'll have a better job.

Your marriage:
Someday you'll meet someone to love and share their life with you. Love between a man and woman is second only to the love of God, but there is one big difference. God's love never changes while our love is very changeable. So please remember commitment in your marriage is more important than love. Commitment will save your marriage when your love dies or until it lives again.

I respect and fear God, so I hate evil, pride, arrogance, corruption, and deceit of any kind. (Prov. 8:13)

Persistence, Faith, and Hard Work Pay

IF YOU'RE a golf fan, you probably saw the Buick Classic on Sunday, June 14, 1998. J. P. Hayes, now officially referred to as "Jackpot Hayes," won the tournament by beating Jim Furyk for his first PGA Tour victory.

As a result, Hayes won $324,000, which was nearly as much as he earned in the previous five years on the Tour. He also won a two-year exemption on the PGA Tour. That was particularly gratifying to J. P. because the following year was the first in eight or nine years that he did not have to fill out an application for qualifying school.

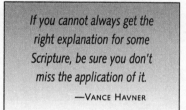

If you cannot always get the right explanation for some Scripture, be sure you don't miss the application of it.

—VANCE HAVNER

No one can possibly imagine the turmoil in his mind as he played the final round, and the relief he experienced as a result of winning the tournament. The grind of struggling for financial and professional survival must have taken its toll, and yet he seemed calm and relaxed at the end of the grueling event. However, he acknowledged that the win hadn't fully hit him, and probably in a few days he would wake up and be even more appreciative of its significance.

I was impressed with the way Hayes handled himself, but even more impressed with the fact that he persisted because he believed he had what it took to be a winner. We'll never know how many people quit with the goal just around the corner; how many kids have missed a scholarship because they did not study just ten more minutes daily; how many more marriages could have been saved if they had made one more effort to make it work.

Even if we do not accomplish all of our objectives, giving it our best shot will guarantee success because winning is not everything, but best effort is. Persistence, faith, and hard work will give everyone rewards that go far beyond a paycheck.

I trust the Lord completely, and not myself, so I have a reputation for good judgment and common sense. (Prov. 3:4–5)

525,600

THERE ARE 525,600 minutes in every year. How do you use those minutes? How many of those minutes do you exercise, or do you use the old excuse, "I just don't have time"?

In his book *Fit for Success*, Dr. James M. Rippe surveyed Fortune 500 CEOs and was surprised to discover that these busy executives were three times more likely than others to exercise. Two-thirds of them engaged in aerobic exercise at least three times a week and said it helped them to reduce stress, increase their energy, improve their health, and boost their productivity.

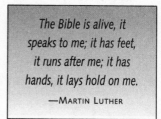

> The Bible is alive, it speaks to me; it has feet, it runs after me; it has hands, it lays hold on me.
> —MARTIN LUTHER

I'm not the CEO of a Fortune 500 company, but I believe I'm as busy as almost anyone. I have found that by maintaining a regular exercise schedule, I have increased my energy level, improved my health, reduced my weight, and lowered my blood pressure, resting heart rate, and cholesterol level.

Nobody asks, "When do you have time to eat?" The answer is obvious: we make the time. Exercise is much the same way. Experts maintain that three twenty-minute walks a week will do wonders for your health. Since I started exercising more than a quarter century ago, my productivity has substantially improved. It's actually made me more aware of my time and helps me to organize it better. Every moment is important, so I don't waste any of them.

I encourage you to put exercise in your daily program. It will improve your health, and you'll be amazed at what it will do for your organizational skills. If you don't plan your time, someone will take it. Plan your time to include exercise, and you'll get more done in every area of your life, which means you will receive more blessings.

I cling to wisdom, so she protects me. I love wisdom, so she guards me. (Prov. 2:2–6)

Music, Movies, and TV Influences

IT'S AN OLD DEBATE, and everybody who disagrees will say we have no anecdotal evidence to substantiate that what kids hear on recordings or see on TV or in the movies has any bearing on whether they act out what they have seen or heard. However, there is mounting evidence that the words and scenes to which children are exposed influence their behavior.

In a movie made by rock singer Michael Hutchence just a few weeks before his suicide, the former INXS lead singer suggested to a young musician that he kill himself to win a place in rock-'n'-roll history. The July 1998 issue of *Details* magazine contained an article quoting the script and Hutchence's character in the movie

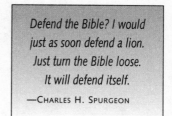

Defend the Bible? I would just as soon defend a lion. Just turn the Bible loose. It will defend itself.

—CHARLES H. SPURGEON

Limp, stating, "Cobain was close. But only because he killed himself," referring to rock star Kurt Cobain. "It was brilliant on his part." Hutchence was found hanging from a noose in a hotel room in Australia.

Chances are good that you have gone to a movie or watched a TV program and either laughed or cried, depending on the portrayal. If what went into your mind from the screen can make you laugh or cry, doesn't it make sense that what goes into your mind from the screen could also cause you to help someone or hurt someone?

Can any serious-minded person really believe that lyrics advocating the raping and mutilation of women, the shooting of policemen, suicide, violence, and other depraved acts do not over a period of time have an impact on the listener? Even if these recordings, movies, or TV shows don't influence people, can you think of any benefits that come from playing such lyrics or showing violence? Eliminate much of the gratuitous sex and violence via the media, and all of us will have a better chance at a happier, healthier, safer future.

I am becoming wise because I am determined to be wise, and I am developing common sense and good judgment. (Prov. 4:7)

Week Twenty-Four

Slow Down for Better Results

NORMAN K. AUGUSTINE, chairman of the executive committee of the Lockheed Martin Corporation, used this little example to get our attention:

> Management cannot adopt the attitude exhibited by a local bus service in rural England, whose drivers passed by long queues of would-be passengers with a smile and a wave of the hand. "It is impossible for the drivers to keep their timetables if they must stop for passengers," explained one of the company's officials. The logic is certainly impeccable, but something seems to have been missed.

This incident probably never happened, but it gives us something to think about when we explore how we can keep our customers happy.

Another favorite story tells of the sales manager who was gung ho about making lots of calls.

> *The Christian who is careless in Bible reading will be careless in Christian living.*
> —MAX I. REICH

He emphasized that if you made the calls, you would make the sales, and he set an unreasonably high number of calls for each salesperson. At the end of the first week one salesman had made more than three hundred calls. The manager was duly impressed and invited the young salesman to stand up and explain how he did it. The salesman shared his secret: "It was really no problem. I could have made even more, except a number of the people stopped me to ask questions."

Don't lose sight of your objective. Use your common sense, and apply yourself. The same principle holds true on any job— as long as you're there, get busy. Who knows? Rewards beyond your wildest expectations might come your way in the form of raises, bonuses, and promotions. Give it a shot. You've got nothing to lose and much to gain.

I am perfect in God's eyes, and He always cares for me in my distress. (Ps. 4:1)

Those Neurotransmitters

PSYCHIATRIST PETER MARZUK, of Cornell University Medical College, did an interesting study concerning the suicide rate among pregnant women. He found that of the 315 New York City women who took their own lives between 1990 and 1993, only 6 were pregnant. He said that was about 70 percent fewer than he'd expect, given the city's pregnancy and suicide demographics.

Dr. Marzuk noted that while there are no doubt psychological factors that help explain the low suicide rate among pregnant women, he also believed that the brain chemical serotonin plays a major role. He reasons that low serotonin levels have been linked to higher risk of depression and impulsive behavior. However, during pregnancy, the baby develops its own serotonin supply, and perhaps the mother feeds off that. He suggested in the *American Journal of Psychiatry* that

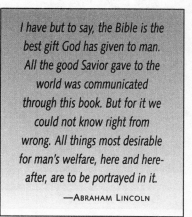

I have but to say, the Bible is the best gift God has given to man. All the good Savior gave to the world was communicated through this book. But for it we could not know right from wrong. All things most desirable for man's welfare, here and here-after, are to be portrayed in it.

—ABRAHAM LINCOLN

whether it's by coincidence or by design, the neurochemical boost helps a baby ensure its survival.

Other studies reveal that listening to inspirational messages from speakers, teachers, or preachers can enhance the flow of serotonin and alleviate some of the stress and reduce the impact of premenstrual syndrome (PMS) in women. The more we learn about our minds and how to stimulate and use them, the more benefits we derive.

The message is clear: if you feed your mind something good and positive, you will reap something good and positive from your mind.

Because I keep on eating the fruit from the tree of wisdom, I am happy. (Prov. 3:18)

Slow Down, Preacher

THE TYPICAL AMERICAN believes that men and women who fill the pulpits in the churches work a few hours on the weekend and probably spend some time visiting folks, preparing sermons, and counseling troubled individuals during the week. In short, they have it pretty easy.

Reality gives us an entirely different picture. According to a study published in *Leadership Journal*, the average evangelical clergyman works more than fifty hours a week, including four evenings, and will take an average of four phone calls at home every night. Forty-two percent of pastors' spouses will complain about the schedule at least once a month. As a result, sometime during the month a typical pastor will feel both physical and emotional stress.

Most pastors work excessive hours voluntarily. Their boards or congregations don't demand such a schedule. They spend about four-

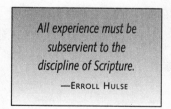

All experience must be subservient to the discipline of Scripture.
—ERROLL HULSE

teen hours each week planning and attending meetings and services, thirteen hours teaching and preparing sermons, nine hours offering pastoral care and counseling, six hours praying and engaging in personal devotions, and thirteen hours taking care of other tasks, which include long-range planning and evangelism. That leaves them precious little time for being with the family and tending to their own physical, mental, emotional, and spiritual needs.

The results speak for themselves. The dropout rate is high. The number who suffer from fatigue, depression, and other problems is higher than average in the population.

What's the message? Remember, my pastoral friend, that you can better serve your God, your family, and your church by first taking care of some of your own needs. You've got to have energy to give it; you've got to have strength to share it. You've got to have the right spirit to convey it to others. This is not a selfish approach. It's a wise approach, and it will give you, God, and your family a better, more effective servant.

Message to church members: pray for and encourage your pastor. Volunteer to serve his family. Take them a hot meal, cut the grass, etc. You'll get better sermons if you do.

I give thanks to God for fellow Christians because it is the right thing to do. (2 Thess. 1:3)

Success in Spite Of . . .

ANGEL GAY'S DOCTORS said she would never walk or run. But she became a pitcher on the Palm Beach Lakes junior varsity softball team.

She has a condition called congenital constriction band syndrome. She was born with a malformed left foot, and her right leg was missing. She has an incredible attitude, however, and continues to set high standards for herself. Even though she is missing the bone that should run from her elbow to her wrist and all but one finger on her right hand, she still performs. She wears a prosthetic right leg that attaches at the knee. Her light-hearted personality, combined with a beautiful sense of humor, helps her overcome many difficulties.

> The man of one book is always formidable; but when that book is the Bible he is irresistible.
>
> —W. M. TAYLOR

Angel had been cheerleading since the second grade when she decided to play softball. With fierce determination—and despite the fact that she couldn't answer her own questions such as how she would hold a glove, hit, catch, throw, and run—she was able to solve many of those problems working with her coach, Bill Wilson.

The youngster was an inspiration to the whole team. Left fielder

April Wiwczaroski said, "She's shown me that whatever I put my heart into I can go get. She's out there running whether it hurts her or not because that's what she wants. She helps us put things into perspective."

Distance running was painful for Angel, but she participated by doing it slowly. Although her base running wasn't the fastest on the team, it wasn't the slowest, either. Not only did Angel Gay give herself a real chance in life, but by her example, she gave her teammates and her community the inspiration to use what they have to be, do, and have more.

God has mercy on me because that is His way with those who love Him. (Ps. 119:132)

Questions Are the Answer

FOR CENTURIES knowledgeable people have recognized that successful leaders have a talent for asking the right questions to get the information they need. They are probing, penetrating, thought-provoking questions that force the other person to think. Doing this enables the leader to bring out the best in that individual.

As individuals, we need to ask ourselves penetrating questions because questions force us to explore our thinking. For example, do you believe your doubts and doubt your beliefs? John L. Mason asks that penetrating question in his book *Ask*, and it really forces you to think. Are you optimistic or pessimistic? Do you lean toward the cynical, or are you open-minded, giving the other person the benefit of the doubt? Do you question everything just to be questioning, or are you intellectually curious, really interested in the answer?

> When you have read the Bible, you will know it is the Word of God because you will have found it the key to your own heart, your own happiness, and your own duty.
> —WOODROW WILSON

Are you preparing yourself for the future, or are you simply waiting for the future? Do you know more about your profession, your family, and yourself today than you did yesterday? What new information or task have you learned? Are you waiting for the future to just happen, or are you taking steps to make certain your future is going to be what you can make it? Do you let your past teach you, or do you let it beat you? Do you recognize that the other person has a point of view and it could well be right, or do you stubbornly push ahead with the iron-clad belief that you've got the answer and refuse to be confused by any compelling evidence that there is a possibility you could be wrong?

Questions really are the answer, and if you ask enough honest ones, you'll end up with a happier, healthier, more fulfilled life.

God's laws are my joyous treasure forever, and I will obey Him forever. (Ps. 119:111)

Week Twenty-Five

When You Thought I Wasn't Looking

AT OUR OFFICE we received a fascinating E-mail message that I thought was so good, I decided to share it with you, and I obtained permission from the author, Mary Rita Schilke Korzan.

When You Thought I Wasn't Looking
When you thought I wasn't looking you hung my first painting on the refrigerator, and I wanted to paint another.

When you thought I wasn't looking you fed a stray cat, and I thought it was good to be kind to animals.

When you thought I wasn't looking you baked a birthday cake just for me, and I knew that little things were special things.

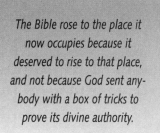

The Bible rose to the place it now occupies because it deserved to rise to that place, and not because God sent anybody with a box of tricks to prove its divine authority.
—BRUCE BARTON

When you thought I wasn't looking you said a prayer, and I believed there was a God that I could always talk to.

When you thought I wasn't looking you kissed me good-night, and I felt loved.

When you thought I wasn't looking I saw tears come from your eyes, and I learned that sometimes things hurt—but that it's all right to cry.

When you thought I wasn't looking you smiled, and it made me want to look that pretty, too.

When you thought I wasn't looking you cared, and I wanted to be everything I could be.

When you thought I wasn't looking—I looked . . . and wanted to say thanks for all those things you did when you thought I wasn't looking.

You can be reasonably sure that whether you realize it or not, someone is looking, and whether it's friend or foe, you will have an impact on whoever is watching when you live with integrity.

My God guides me with His laws so I will not be overcome by evil. (Ps. 119:133)

Message from an Olympian

MATT GHAFFARI, an immigrant from Iran who won the silver medal in Greco-Roman wrestling in the 1996 Olympic Games and has been the U.S. national amateur wrestling champ for the last seven years, addressed our company and gave us sound advice.

He reminded us that we awaken to an "opportunity" clock and not an "alarm" clock. He pointed out that the opportunity clock rings every day, and winners always answer it, mediocre individuals periodically answer it, and losers never awaken to the opportunity that is theirs here in America. Matt advised us that in all the Olympic sports, the average length of time it takes an athlete to win a gold medal is fifteen years. Virtually every gold medal winner always keeps his goals in his pocket so he can constantly refer to them. The athletes eat, sleep, drink, and dream about winning a gold medal. He observed that anyone with the same commitment to excellence would go much farther in life.

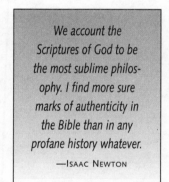

We account the Scriptures of God to be the most sublime philosophy. I find more sure marks of authenticity in the Bible than in any profane history whatever.

—ISAAC NEWTON

Matt, a strong family man and a man of deep faith, believes

you have to be a human being first and a sports person second. He believes Olympic athletes with families must organize their training around their family commitments because family goals are fully as important as—perhaps even more important than— any other goal.

As a result of his philosophy, Matt is doing much with his life, and if we will follow his example, we will be able to do much with ours.

I belong to Christ, and He has nailed my natural evil desires to His cross and crucified them there. (Gal. 5:24)

A Teamwork Dilemma

I SUSPECT that all of us in the worlds of business, athletics, music, and other professions recognize the importance of teamwork. Old clichés come to mind: "Individuals score points, but teams win games."

In the business world the concept of teamwork is particularly important, but according to Ed Petry, executive director of the Ethics Officer Association in Belmont, Massachusetts, one dilemma regularly confronts teams working in a business together. The dilemma is one of ethics or integrity. Petry pointed out in a February 17, 1998, article in *USA Today* that when you work in a team and become close to the other members, it often happens

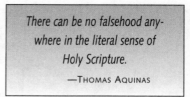

There can be no falsehood anywhere in the literal sense of Holy Scripture.

—THOMAS AQUINAS

that an individual engages in unethical conduct, whether it's taking money or revealing trade secrets. The question is, Do you tell the boss? He noted that if you tell, working well in a small group becomes harder to do. According to Graham Phaup at the Institute for Global Ethics in Camden, Maine, "It's truth vs. loyalty. Is it right to tell the truth and lose friendships?" Those who report problems, he said, risk being shunned by others on their team if word gets out. Managers say they strive to let workers know they should tell when something is amiss.

It really is a dilemma, and this is the point where the integrity of management is critical in solving the problem. If the workers know that they can talk with complete confidence to people in management and that their trust will never be betrayed, they are far more likely to report a situation that could potentially be job threatening for all of them. That's integrity, and that's a quality we all need to develop and maintain every day.

I stay pure by obeying Your Word and following its rules. (Ps. 119:9)

George Was a Hero

IN THIS DAY of the antihero, when the public and the media seem to take delight in promoting people like Howard Stern and Marilyn Manson (and much of the population embraces them), it's refreshing to look at George Washington and the reason for his greatness.

Early in his life Washington was exposed to some of the remarkable moral philosophy of the time. Richard Brookhiser edited and offered a commentary on a book by George Washington, *Rules of Civility*. The subtitle explains the topic: *The 110*

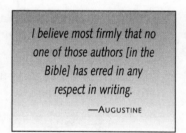

I believe most firmly that no one of those authors [in the Bible] has erred in any respect in writing.

—AUGUSTINE

Precepts That Guided Our First President in War and Peace. Here are some examples from that book:

- Use no reproachable language against any one, neither curse nor revile.

- Associate yourself with men of good quality if you esteem your own reputation; for 'tis better to be alone than in bad company.

- Be not hasty to believe flying reports to the disparagement of any.

- Speak not injurious words neither in jest nor earnest; scoff at none although they give occasion.

- Think before you speak, pronounce not imperfectly, nor bring out your words too hastily, but orderly, distinctly.

- Be not curious to know the affairs of others, neither approach those that speak in private.

- Speak not evil of the absent for it is unjust.

- Drink not nor talk with your mouth full, neither gaze about you while you are dining.

- When you speak of God or His attributes, let it be seriously and with reverence. Honor and obey your natural parents though they be poor.

- Labor to keep alive in your breast that little spark of celestial fire called conscience.

Obviously there are many more rules, but that's a pretty solid foundation upon which you can build a life and a career, and become a healthy role model.

———————————————

I have thought much about your words and stored them in my heart so they would hold me back from sin. (Ps. 119:11)

Example: The Best Teacher

THIS LITTLE POEM crossed my desk recently, and it exposed a great truth:

> I lost a very little word
> Just the other day,
> It was a very naughty word
> I had not meant to say.
> But then, it was not really lost
> When from my lips it flew,
> My little daughter picked it up
> And now she says it, too.

"Out of the mouths of babes come words their parents wish they had never said." We teach by example, of this there is no doubt. The parent who preaches one thing and practices another is sending mixed signals to the child, and this often leads to confusion. Very few people verbally instruct their children to lie, cheat, steal, and/or behave violently. Seldom does a parent say to a child, "Now

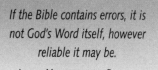

If the Bible contains errors, it is not God's Word itself, however reliable it may be.
—JAMES MONTGOMERY BOICE

Johnny (or Susie), you're four years old, and it's time you started learning some 'adult' language. Here are the words to use when you are angry or irritated or want to impress someone with your 'savvy' and street smarts. Cussword number one in the introductory course to vile language is . . . ," and then proceed to teach word by word all of the things we should neither say nor hear.

No, that's not the way the parents do it. The child overhears the parents' language, and then for some strange reason the parents are embarrassed when the child uses language he is only repeating from them. It's more than just a cliché to say a child won't believe everything you say, but he will believe everything you do.

Use lots of four-letter words such as *good, real, fair, hope,* and *love.* Include volumes of adult language such as *integrity, commitment,* and *responsibility,* and you will have a well-spoken child you will be proud of.

I have chosen to be faithful so I cling to Your commands and follow them as closely as I can. (Ps. 119:30)

Week Twenty-Six

He Didn't Forget

A FEW YEARS before the end of the fifteenth century, two young friends, Albrecht Dürer and Franz Knigstein, were struggling young artists. They were very poor and worked to support themselves while they studied art. Things were tough, and work took so much of their time that their advancement was slow. Finally, they reached an agreement and decided to draw lots. One of them would work to support both of them while the other studied art.

Albrecht won, so he studied art full-time while Franz worked at hard labor. They agreed that when Albrecht was successful, he would support Franz, who would then study art. Albrecht went off to the art centers of Europe to study. As many people now know, he had not only talent but also genius. When he had attained his success, he went back to keep his bargain with Franz. Much to his chagrin, he discovered the enormous price his friend had paid. The hard manual labor

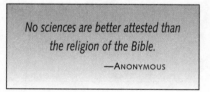

No sciences are better attested than the religion of the Bible.

—ANONYMOUS

had made Franz's fingers twisted and stiff, and he could no longer make the delicate brush strokes that fine art required. Though his artistic dreams could never be realized, Franz was not embittered; rather, he rejoiced in his friend's success.

One day Dürer found Knigstein kneeling with his gnarled hands intertwined in prayer, quietly praying for the success of his friend. He hurriedly sketched the folded hands of his faithful friend and later completed the truly great masterpiece known the world over as *The Praying Hands*.

Today many art galleries feature Albrecht Dürer's works. But none of his other works hold the place in the hearts of people that *The Praying Hands* does. It tells an eloquent story of sacrifice, labor, gratitude, and love.

Tell me what to do, Lord, and I will do it. As long as I live, I'll wholeheartedly obey. (Ps. 119:33–34)

It Takes Time

"I INTENDED to call you last week, but got busy and time slipped through my fingers." "I would love to take a couple of days to visit my folks, but the time just doesn't exist." Have you heard or said something like this lately?

Regardless of how busy we are, we need to take time for ten things.

1. We need to take time to work because it is the price of success.

> *Our faith is fed by what is plain in Scripture and tried by what is obscure.*
> —AUGUSTINE

2. We need to take time to think because it is the source of power and the key to making good decisions.

3. We need to take time to play because it is the secret of youth, and all work does make a person dull.

4. We need to take time to read because it is the foundation of knowledge.

5. We need to take time to worship because it is the highway of reverence and washes the dust of the earth from our eyes.

6. We need to take time to help and enjoy friends because our friends ultimately are going to be a major source of comfort and happiness.

7. We need to take time to love because it is the sacrament of life that might be the most important—and yet the most missed—element in our lives.

8. We need to take time to dream because it is the foundation upon which hope is built.

9. We need to take time to laugh. It has been called the "music of the soul."

10. We need to take time to plan. It's the secret of being able to have time for the first nine things.

— Anonymous

We need to remember that the things that can't be counted are the things that count the most. Follow these steps and you will enjoy a balanced life.

I prefer being obedient to making money, and I want God's plan because His promises are for me, for I trust and revere Him. (Ps. 119:36–38)

Life Is an Attitude

RON HEAGY is an outstanding author, speaker, and counselor who has his master's degree in social counseling. He is also a mouth painter and has sold more than a thousand pictures. He has been happily married since 1992 to a loving and beautiful wife.

To see Ron is an inspiration. To listen to him is an encouragement. To read him is educational. He developed all his skills and accomplished all these objectives after he broke his neck in a surfing accident that left him a quadriplegic. Today his most outstanding characteristic is his tremendously good attitude. Meeting him and looking into his eyes, watching his video, and reading his book, *Life Is an Attitude*, are inspiring experiences. As he expresses it, "Attitudes are contagious. Is yours worth catching?"

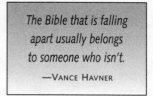

The Bible that is falling apart usually belongs to someone who isn't.

—VANCE HAVNER

Before the accident Ron was an outstanding high school athlete who had a scholarship to play football at Oregon State University. He was injured on the day before his eighteenth birthday. One day he could bench-press three hundred pounds; the next day he couldn't lift his finger. In the early days following the accident, Ron was heartbroken, angry, and bitter, and he held more than a few pity parties as he grieved his losses.

Fortunately for Ron, his mother, an upbeat woman who loves him deeply, encouraged him to develop his other talents and abilities, and suggested that he become a painter.

Eventually he could lift his voice *and* his paintbrush with his mouth. Now Ron travels the country encouraging people to use what they have to help others have a better life. Ron's accomplishments are an inspiration to all of us. Take Ron Heagy's approach, and you will be more, do more, and have more of what life has to offer.

I praise the Lord for He loves me dearly and His faithfulness endures. (Ps. 117:1–2)

This Way to a Promotion

IT'S SAFE to say that everyone who reads this and works for someone else would accept an increase in income if it was offered. However, many would accept the increase in income, hoping there would be no increase in responsibilities, which is not a realistic attitude. In most cases, promotions are given because of past efforts and future expectations. It is the managers' way of saying, "We value you. We want to keep you around for the future because in the past you have performed better than good."

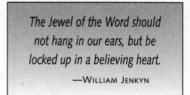

The Jewel of the Word should not hang in our ears, but be locked up in a believing heart.
—WILLIAM JENKYN

How do you get that raise or promotion? First, you need to arrive a few minutes early each day. It's amazing what a fifteen-minute early arrival will do for your productivity. It gets you off to the right start, and the employer notices. It's much better to arrive early than it is to stay late because, on occasion, the question might arise about whether it takes you longer than necessary to fulfill your responsibilities. Not always, of course, but there is that possibility.

Next, you need to handle each assignment as if a promotion depended on it. Obviously, each assignment does not automatically lead to a promotion; however, the cumulative effect is substantial. When you give each job your best shot, you will establish a positive reputation, which is good security and promotion insurance.

Then, you need to display excitement and enthusiasm for what you do, and let both be reflected by the smile on your face. A pleasant demeanor and an upbeat attitude, combined with increasing your knowledge and improving your skill level, are highly desirable.

These basic little approaches will give your boss—and eventually you—happiness.

I pray and God answers and saves me from my distress. (Ps. 118:5)

The Way to a Woman's Heart

THIS ADVICE WILL probably stun most readers—particularly male readers—but the way to your wife's heart is through your ear. When you listen to her and treat what she has to say with respect, you do more for her self-esteem than you could with the gifts you might bring her to apologize for being late for dinner the last three evenings. And when she feels good about herself, it's easier for her to feel good about you.

A survey of 1,744 men and women revealed that 44 percent of the women said the listening ear was more effective in helping them appreciate their own abilities than any gift, while 48 percent of the men in this survey said their self-esteem grew when they helped their wives with their problems. Conclusion: when the husband listened to what his wife had to say, both won. She felt good because he listened, and he felt good because she felt good and took the appropriate action if any was required.

> Pause at every verse of Scripture and shake, as it were, every bough of it, that if possible some fruit at least may drop down.
>
> —MARTIN LUTHER

To continue with the irony of this information, 53 percent of the women said they do not get all the emotional support they need from their marital or romantic relationships. In short, the men are not listening and more than half the women are unhappy because of that. On the other side of the scale, 65 percent of the men believe they are getting the emotional support they need from their mates.

It's really ironic, isn't it, that the solution to most problems is courteously listening and then taking appropriate action? Think about that. Listen more carefully, and you and your mate will have a happier, more intimate relationship.

God is my strength and song in the heat of battle, and He gives me victory. (Ps. 118:14)

About the Author

Zig Ziglar is the chairman of Zig Ziglar Corporation, which is committed to helping people more fully utilize their physical, mental, and spiritual resources. Ziglar is one of the most sought-after inspirational speakers in the country. He travels around the world delivering his message of hope, humor, and enthusiasm to audiences of all kinds and sizes.

Ziglar is the best-selling author of many books, including *Confessions of a Grieving Christian*, *Confessions of a Happy Christian*, *Something to Smile About*, *Over the Top*, and *See You at the Top*, which has sold more than 1.5 million copies worldwide. He and his wife, Jean, make their home in Dallas, Texas.

More Best-Selling Books by Zig Ziglar

Confessions of a Grieving Christian
In this uplifting book, Zig Ziglar uses the experience of losing his oldest daughter, Suzan, to encourage you to deal with the reality of loss and learn to take up the threads of life again as you find consolation and inspiration in the Giver of All Peace.
0-8407-9182-8 • Hardcover • 288 pages

Over the Top—Revised and Updated
This sequel to the best-seller *See You at the Top* has been revised and updated with pages full of on-target advice for maximum success and happiness. Ziglar identifies and shows precisely how to achieve what everyone desires most in life—to be happy, healthy, reasonably prosperous, and secure and to have friends, peace of mind, good family relationships, and hope.
0-7852-7119-8 • Hardcover • 336 pages

Something to Smile About
The inspiring stories in this book will give you a daily word of encouragement, which Zig Ziglar calls "the fuel of hope." They will also give you something to smile about and, on occasion, even a healthy laugh.
0-8407-9183-6 • Hardcover • 224 pages

Something *Else* to Smile About

In the tradition of *Something to Smile About,* Zig Ziglar returns with another inspiring collection of masterfully told stories from his own life and the lives of others. Humorous anecdotes, poignant encounters, and touching narratives breathe life into lessons on character, leaving a legacy, true greatness, personal integrity, and overcoming adversity.

Whether you need a morning shot of ambition or a refreshing thought before a good night's sleep, *Something* Else *to Smile About* is a daily source of motivation and encouragement you'll turn to again and again and enthusiastically share with others.
0-7852-9612-6 • Hardcover • 224 pages

Courtship After Marriage

Master motivational teacher Zig Ziglar champions romantic commitments in his new here's-how-to-do-it-*right!* guide to happily ever after. Just how important is marriage? Zig Ziglar thinks it is so important that he has constructed a six-step process to keep the commitment in marriage—or how to get it back if you've lost it. (And if this is your second go round at marriage, you can make sure this one lasts a lifetime.)

Good advice, homespun stories, challenging data, and practical applications are combined in this zesty tribute to a romantic marriage that lasts.
0-8407-9111-9 • Hardcover • 256 pages